A SAFE PLACE

A SAFE PLACE

LUIS D. APONTE

Copyright

Copyright © 2025 by Luis D. Aponte

Book cover design by David Provolo.

eBooks available on Smashwords.com.

Physical books available on IngramSpark.com.

Audiobook available on major platforms via Voices by INaudio.

For more information, go to www.ASafePlaceBook.com.

All rights reserved. No part of this book may be reproduced in any manner whatsoever without written permission except in the case of brief quotations embodied in critical articles and reviews.

Paperback ISBN-13: 979-8-9910989-5-3
eBook ISBN-13 (ePub): 979-8-9910989-0-8
eAudiobook ISBN-13: 979-8-9910989-4-6
Library of Congress Control Number: 2025911115

Owl & Scroll Publishers ♦ Manassas, Virginia

Dedication

This book is dedicated to my sister—a special education teacher, wife, mother and grandmother—who took her own life with a firearm on October 31, 2022. It also is written in honor of my alma mater, Marjory Stoneman Douglas High School, which suffered the worst school shooting in Florida's history on February 14, 2018. Lastly, the countless victims of gun violence in schools—those who are no longer with us, as well as the family members and friends who still suffer every day from the wake of its rippling effect—this book is dedicated to you.

My hope is that this book will help bring us together in order to help save lives. Children and educators deserve to feel safe in schools without the threat of gun violence.

Contents

Copyright		v
Dedication		vi
Special Thank You		ix
Foreword		xi
Marjory Stoneman Douglas High School		xiii
Parkland Strong		xiv
1	The Four Deaths	1
2	Good Trouble	11
3	Bookmarks in Life	14
4	Superhero Parents Emerge From Gun Violence	24
5	Everyone in the Community Has a Role	30
6	Understanding School Gun Violence	34
7	30 Years of School Shooting Trends	50
8	Roots and Myths Behind Motivations	59
9	Overlooked Warning Signs	66
10	Most Vulnerable Locations	73
11	Mass vs. Conventional School Shootings	85
12	How to Prevent the Next School Shooting	98
13	To Ban or Not to Ban AR-15s	141
14	Alyssa's Law	145

15 Stand for the Silent	150
16 Apps That Can Help Save Children's Lives	155
17 A Positive Note	158
About the Author	162
Connect With Me	164
Other Titles by Luis D. Aponte	165
Book Discussion Guide	167
Notes	169
Chapter Sample of Author's Next Book	184

Special Thank You

The documentation featured within this book and within *The Ultimate U.S. School Shooting Reference Guide, Volumes 1-3* would not have been possible without the endless support and encouragement of my loving wife, Eileen; the tireless diligence of thousands of journalists and authors; the resourcefulness of dozens of research librarians across the country fulfilling my information requests; and the brilliant teams behind Newspapers.com, NewsBank, Gun Violence Archive, Everytown for Gun Safety, the Naval Postgraduate School Center for Homeland Defense and Security, GunMemorial.org, the National School Safety Center, Citizens Crime Commission of New York City, Ballotpedia, Eric Laurine of the School Shooting Database, several law enforcement agencies, coroner's offices, public court documents, the U.S. House of Representatives Subcommittee on Early Childhood, Youth and Families; as well as the Founding Fathers of the United States, who believed, "Our liberty depends on the freedom of the press, and that cannot be limited without being lost." ~ Thomas Jefferson, 1786

Special thanks to Emily Taffel-Cohen of Mugsy PR for your expert book launching advice; Research Librarian Michelle Quigley, who created data heat maps of my results; my talented book cover designer, David Provolo; infographic designer, Harrison Snell; editors, John DeChancie and Andy Beth Miller; and beta readers Maryam Nawaz and Melanie Green. You are all worth your weight in gold!

Finally, heartfelt thanks to Lori Alhadeff and Kirk Smalley for generously sharing your stories with me and for your tireless, selfless work in saving lives every day. Your dedication is truly inspirational. As a token of my gratitude, fifty percent of all profits from this book and *The Ultimate U.S. School Shooting Reference Guide, Volumes 1-3* will be donated to your nonprofit organizations, Make Our Schools Safe and Stand for the Silent.

Your collective efforts and expertise help made a positive impact in this world. Thank you!

Foreword

Bethany Pitchford, Ph.D., Assistant Professor of Business Communications, Department of Business Administration and Entrepreneurship, Sam Houston State University

My silences had not protected me.
Your silence will not protect you.
- Audre Lorde

"Listen," my sister says as soon as I answer the phone.
"Yes?" I respond.
"I need you to stay calm. Our family is safe. But you should know that there's a mass shooting happening in Odessa right now."

August 31st, 2019, changed everyone's lives whether we were directly affected by the violence or not. Nobody expects to have a conversation like this because gun violence is elsewhere. It can't happen here, to me, to my people. But the thing is, gun violence doesn't discriminate and could happen to anyone.

Essentially, *A Safe Place* is Luis Aponte's call to action for every American to stand up and take non-partisan, holistic steps to end this epidemic before they lose someone they love. Grounded in seven years of credible research, data gathering, and analysis, Aponte provides a detailed overview of helpful steps to take such as safe gun storage, consistent metal detector use, increased numbers of school security guards and counselors, and anti-bullying/emotional management campaigns. Parents can also play a role by monitoring their child's media and phone use and helping kids understand how to deal with emotional situations in healthy ways. And every community member can help by speaking up if they see something that looks off. Sometimes all it takes to turn things around and prevent more violence is letting people who are struggling know that someone cares about them, it's okay to talk about mental illness, and help is available. Silence doesn't save lives.

I first met Luis via a mutual friend, Dr. Shera Jackson, when I was a doctoral student in Media and Communication at Texas Tech University. My research focuses on how journalists frame mental illness when reporting on mass shootings. Previous research shows most people with mental illness are not violent, and negative news frames increase stigma, which can prevent people from getting the help they need. My goal is to work with journalists to better understand why these negative news frames continue to occur so that maybe, over time, the number of negative frames and stigma can decrease to help people receive vital treatment.

When Shera heard about my dissertation study, she told me about Luis and his research. She also showed me the portraits he paints of the victims, and then I reached out to connect with him. Knowing someone with similar research interests has been vital to continuing my own work.

In *A Safe Place*, Luis doesn't just discuss the fact that gun violence is an American epidemic. He provides concrete steps everyone can take to help solve this problem. He reminds readers that "We do not have time to be bothered with the petty differences of politics, race, religion, and social status. Now is the time to recognize fact from fiction. Our survival literally depends on it."

And if we're all going to survive, now is the time to stand up, speak up, and keep fighting for our lives. We deserve to live.

Marjory Stoneman Douglas High School

Marjory Stoneman Douglas High School, Parkland, Florida
Photo by Luis D. Aponte

Marjory Stoneman Douglas High School in Parkland, Florida on March 2, 2018 – approximately two weeks after the worst mass school shooting in Florida's history on February 14, 2018.

Parkland Strong

Parkland Strong Banner
Photo by Luis D. Aponte

One of many banners posted by students and communities from across the United States on the outer fence border of Marjory Stoneman Douglas High School in 2018 in Parkland, Florida. This banner features the 17 victims who lost their lives during the Parkland mass shooting.

1

The Four Deaths

Operator: "9-1-1, what is your emergency?"
Caller: "Hi, my daughter just texted me from school...She says there's an active shooter!"

Imagine the visceral panic a parent feels when their child is in mortal danger. Adrenaline surges through their veins, causing their heartbeat to accelerate and their breaths to shorten. Fear grips their chest as every worst-case scenario races through their mind. Primal instincts to act swiftly and fiercely overwhelm all other senses. Every cell in their body is intensely focused on protecting the life of their precious loved one. Too many communities believe a school shooting could never happen to them...until it does.

No fear or pain on Earth is greater for a parent than that of losing their child. I recently read that the Ancient Egyptians believed we die twice: first, when we take our final breath; and second, when our name is spoken for the last time. In my own family, at least four relatives have endured the unimaginable loss of their own children—one to a car accident, one to a heart arrhythmia, and two to gun violence.

Based on the long, aching grief that followed, I've come to believe that parents who mourn the loss of a child suffer not two, but four deaths. The first comes vicariously, with the death of their child. The second strikes emotionally, as they lay their beloved to rest. The third arrives physically when they themselves pass away. And the forth is metaphysical when both the parent and child are forgotten by history, echoing the belief of the Ancient Egyptians. To break this tragic cycle, we must remember their stories and the lessons they teach. These lessons should first be embraced by educators and parents, then openly discussed within their communities, and ultimately reflected in school policies. Through the research in this book and *The Ultimate U.S. School Shooting Reference Guide, Volumes 1-3*, my goal is to help prevent such heartbreak for as many families as possible. Above all, these lessons must never be forgotten, ensuring that this painful history is never repeated.

In an effort to prevent future tragedies and honor the memories of those affected, this book and *The Ultimate U.S. School Shooting Reference Guide, Volumes 1-3* include the names of both victims and perpetrators. This decision is made with the utmost respect for the lives lost and the profound impact on their families and communities. By including these names, it is my aim to educate readers about the human toll of these tragic events, inspire meaningful change, and support future researchers in expanding upon this work. It is through remembering and acknowledging these individuals that we can truly understand the gravity of the issue and work together toward a safer future for all.

This exclusive circle of hell is understood in every culture in the world. Thousands of young victims are among the casualties of those bombed by foreign military forces in countries like Ukraine, Palestine, Israel, Syria, Afghanistan, and Iraq. South American refugees' children have drowned or starved to death while trying to escape war and persecution in Venezuela, Honduras, El Salvador, Guatemala, and Mexico. Finally, thousands of instruments of death exist here in the United States, and they also claim the lives of many children. These instruments include human trafficking, distracted driving, drug abuse, suicide, gang violence, and of course, gun violence. If society keeps experiencing the same failures, it is because we have failed to learn from the mistakes of our history. I believe we're missing a crucial book in stores and libraries—one that provides practical solutions that communities and schools can implement themselves. Everyone is so frustrated with "the waiting" and the "thoughts and prayers." My hope? This book, guided by experts, fills that void for you and your community.

I can imagine no greater agony or rage than having to bury one's own child. Although I have no children of my own, I recently experienced the loss of my sister on my father's side of my family—a school teacher who committed suicide with a firearm on October 31, 2022. My family is still struggling with the pain and unanswered questions each day. As the eldest sibling on my mother's side, who had to pitch in to help care for the younger members of my family, I still remember gently swaying my infant brother in a wooden rocking chair while feeding him a bottle and then happily watching him sleep peacefully as his protective big brother. Today, my brother is a former U.S. Marine with children of his own who are now in college. I would protect each of my siblings with my own life. Each memory, from the first moment a parent holds their newborn baby in the palm of their hands and gasps in awe and adoration, to the last "I love you" exchanged before their child walks out the front door to a life of their own, can become like heavy boulders crushing a parent's heart if that child should ever die. I know this emotional, psychological, and spiritual weight can break even the most hardened soldier and crush the very core of being.

It is often difficult to identify a single powerful moment in our youth that may have dramatically influenced our forged path into adulthood. My personal moment was the day the threat of gun violence immediately canceled the dreams I had once imagined for my life and forced me to make a decision to leave high school one year early. On that fateful day, I was oblivious to the other students around me as I walked through the Marjory Stoneman Douglas High School's main courtyard in Parkland, enjoying the warmth of the South Florida sun. It was the fall of my junior year, and I was feeling a little taller because I had finally stood up to a bully in my Oceanography class just the day before. That very morning, a Korean friend of mine ran toward me just as the morning school bell rang, indicating we needed to be in class. He declared,

"David, you need to leave school now!" I went by my middle name back then because kids used to make fun of my traditional Hispanic first name, Luis.

"Why?" I asked.

"(That guy) is looking for you, and he has a gun," my friend warned.

Perhaps embarrassing a convicted drug dealer in front of his gang member friends had not been one of my best life decisions. My illusion then was that too many people got shot because they didn't know when to walk away or when to shut up. That day, I decided, was not going to be one of those days. I was not about to test my tournament martial arts skills against a convicted drug dealer who was looking for me with a gun. *Walk away, David. Don't ever come back* was what my common sense demanded.

I often think about that day in 1993 when I left high school a year early. It seemed necessary then to avoid being shot and possibly even killed. Most teens look forward to every rite of passage—prom, graduation, a girlfriend, and maybe a baseball scholarship—so my recently divorced mother, who was on welfare with four children, wouldn't have to worry about helping to pay for my college aspirations. All these, however, were suddenly only wishful dreams. Still, I also knew that if I had stayed in school, I might not be alive right now. I never imagined then that three decades later, I would be writing a book inspired by the worst school shooting in Florida's history that took place at my old high school. To this day, I still don't understand why a convicted drug dealer with a known gang affiliation was allowed to attend a conventional high school and why I was the one who was forced to complete my education from home because he decided to bring a gun to school. Thankfully, I didn't give him the chance to use it on me.

When the news broke of the mass shooting on February 14, 2018 at my alma mater, Marjory Stoneman Douglas High School, in Parkland, Florida, I felt paralyzed, angry, and emotionally shredded for all the kids and families who had been affected so horribly and needlessly. In my mind, I had to find a way to bypass the common questions that never get fully answered about any school shooting: "How could this happen here?" "Why was this person allowed to have a gun?" and "How can our politicians sit and do nothing to stop this plague that is spreading in our country?"

I was haunted daily by the images and stories of the Parkland shooting that were appearing in the media. My wife tried to console me as I shook with anger and tears, desperately trying not to destroy the inanimate objects within my reach. Families were screaming for their deceased children once again, and this time it had happened at my own former high school. With predictable precision, politicians started squabbling with each other, blaming the failures of mental health, law enforcement, the school system, violent movies, and video games for the terrorist attack on my old high school. Make no mistake, however, the Parkland mass shooting was a terrorist attack, just like the Covenant Christian School mass shooting in Nashville, Tennessee on March 23, 2023; the Colorado Springs LGBTQ nightclub mass shooting on November 19, 2022; the Robb Elementary School shooting on May 24, 2022; the First Baptist Church mass shooting in Sutherland Springs, Texas, on November 5, 2017; the Las Vegas music festival mass shooting on October 1, 2017; the Orlando Pulse nightclub mass shooting on June 12, 2016; the Sandy Hook Elementary School mass shooting on December 14, 2012; and so many others. However, none of these shootings were being treated as an act of terror should be.

On March 24, 2018, I participated in the peaceful March for Our Lives protest in West Palm Beach, Florida held to honor and support the 17 victims and 17 others injured in the Parkland mass shooting. The march began on Southern Boulevard and ended at the Intracoastal Waterway, just before the bridge at South Flagler Drive that leads directly to Palm Beach—home to the Mar-a-Lago Club and at least 58 billionaires on *Forbes'* list of the world's wealthiest people.[1] Strangely, Palm Beach County Sheriff officers warned us that crossing the bridge would leave us beyond their protection. Simultaneously, over 800 marches took place across the U.S. and worldwide, including in London, Paris, Copenhagen, Madrid, Tokyo, Brisbane, and Rome.[2] Reports poured in as approximately 800,000 protesters gathered in Washington, D.C., while 3,000 marched in West Palm Beach. Being part of the peaceful March for Our Lives event was a privilege and a pivotal part of the American experience. I was deeply impressed by the drive, motivation, and power of this younger generation. This was a historic moment that motivated me to use the power of the written word to support their cause.

After the New York terrorist attacks on September 11, 2001, our government deployed thousands of U.S soldiers, including my younger brother, who served in the U.S. Marine Corps infantry, into a multi-trillion-dollar war for 20 years in Iraq and Afghanistan. After the Parkland mass shooting, however, the politicians simply regurgitated the same cold, emotionless speeches, sort of like pull-string plastic dolls that had only two messages: "...thoughts and prayers" and "This is not a time to talk about gun control." A few politicians and talk show hosts launched vicious conspiracy theory campaigns by claiming the mass shootings were "staged." Imagine the disproportionate political response if the school shooter were brown-skinned, Muslim, gay, transgender, or an undocumented immigrant. We can no longer stand by quietly and do nothing. This is not acceptable in my United States of America. It is our turn to take action and take that action now.

Gun violence in our schools is a crisis that demands our immediate and unwavering attention. The truth is that we have all failed in some measure to prevent this tragedy. I am at fault for not taking action or becoming actively involved until a mass shooting occurred in my old hometown. Perhaps the greatest injustice is remaining silent about the suffering and inequality faced by our neighbors, simply because we believe it doesn't affect us—until it does. Relying on others to solve the problem is not enough. I am guilty of this and hope to address it with the earnest, nonpartisan intention of my research. The echoes of gunfire in school hallways and parking lots are a chilling reminder of our collective failure to protect our children. The media plays an indirect role, as publicizing shootings can lead to copycat incidents, with marginalized individuals seeking notoriety through evil, cruel, and cowardly actions. Nonetheless, when a shooting occurs, society demands to know who, what, when, where, why, and how it happened. It is a Catch-22 paradox.

Schools are at fault because they do not consistently use metal detectors; often lack armed security in parking lots; are vulnerable to multiple entry points; and may have lenient policies that do not enforce any punishments for violations and crimes that are committed on campus as potential warning signs before a shooting. After many of the school shooting incidents in the past three decades, a school spokesperson has often released sterilized public statements that suggest that theirs was just "an isolated event"—as if that comment alone is supposed to pacify the rage and panic that parents feel when they expect their children to be safe in school every day. Law enforcement officers, teachers, parents, and community leaders are often at fault because they may not have strong enough relationships with a significant network of students to identify the warning signs and prevent potential acts of school gun violence before they happen.

Finally, political representatives are habitually at fault due to the financial and social leverage of lobbyists, the 1996 Dickey Amendment that prevented the funding of gun violence research for decades,[3] and the fear of losing power. These factors often handicap their ability and willingness to make meaningful change by applying independently researched and fact-based policies that could actually prevent future shootings. A perfect example is blaming school shootings on mental illness. In my research, only 53 suspects in 1,204 school shootings were reportedly diagnosed with a mental illness, and reporting from only 14 incidents identified mental illness as the motivating factor. That equates to about 1.2%, yet mental illness always seems to grab the headlines of gun violence reports, despite being a rare outlier variable. These failings lead to predictable social media posts of "thoughts and prayers" and accusations toward industries (video games, movies, rock and rap music) that do not have a well-funded lobby actively walking the halls of Congress to defend their financial interests. It is long past time to seek the truth earnestly by investigating the invasive root of gun violence that has uprooted the sanctuary of our educational institutions and the successful learning that should be taking place in them.

Max Eden and Andrew Pollack, the father of Meadow, a student who died in the Parkland shooting, reveal in their book *Why Meadow Died* how school safety policies pressure teachers to reduce discipline numbers by not enforcing rules or by not recording infractions.[4] They argue that this failure to enforce rules and arrest the shooter during his younger years enabled him to acquire the weapon that ended 17 lives and injured 17 others. A critical question arises: Should students face consequences for early misbehavior to prevent escalation, especially given the current lack of accountability for both students and their parents?

In Broward County, Florida, the PROMISE program aims to provide an alternative to arresting students for certain misdemeanors. However, some parents, including Mr. Pollack, blame the program for failing to protect his daughter in the Parkland shooting. On April 21, 2021, Broward Schools Superintendent Robert Runcie was arrested and charged with perjury in South Florida.[5] The indictment claimed Runcie gave false testimony before the Grand Jury, focusing on "whether refusal or failure to follow the mandates of school-related safety laws, such as the *Marjory Stoneman Douglas Public Safety Act*, results in unnecessary and avoidable risk to students across the state."[6] Runcie, the same Superintendent who labeled criticisms of the

PROMISE program as "fake news" in 2018,[7] now faces scrutiny over his actions.

In my research and reflected in *The Ultimate U.S. School Shooting Reference Guide: Volumes 1-3*, I found that schools rarely use their metal detectors, despite owning the equipment. Additionally, the majority of school shootings occur outdoors. Therefore, it is critical for schools to station trained and armed resource officers and security guards in parking lots throughout the day, both during and after school hours, as well as at every extracurricular school activity.

School officials often publicly claim that metal detectors are not used daily due to cost, time, multiple entry points, and the desire to avoid a "prison-like" atmosphere.[8,9,10,11,12] However, airports, courthouses, and sports stadiums manage to avoid this negative perception while using metal detectors consistently. Why, then, are tourists, attorneys, and athletes considered more important than our children and their teachers? This pressing question demands more discussion, reflection, and action.

After the Parkland mass shooting, I began documenting every school shooting in the U.S. from 1990 to 2019 that resulted in injuries or fatalities. The patterns I discovered convinced me that communities can save lives by coming together and collectively addressing the roots of gun violence. The students at Marjory Stoneman Douglas High understood this fundamental truth and ignited a powerful youth movement. Emma González and other survivors of the 2018 Valentine's Day massacre held government officials accountable, and people listened. Thousands of students walked out, and nearly a million people marched peacefully in Washington, D.C., with solidarity marches worldwide. Despite limited media attention for some survivors, a new, infectious energy emerged. These students' unity behind a single message is admirable and inspiring. However, a single strategy may not suffice to prevent future shootings. A fully funded, transparent, and comprehensive study, with publicly available results, followed by bipartisan community action, is essential.

What changed? What triggered millions to unite for justice? This national outrage didn't follow Columbine in 1999, Sandy Hook in 2012, the Orlando Pulse Night Club in 2016, or even the Las Vegas massacre in 2017. Was the tipping point the sheer number of children and teachers killed and injured? Did it happen because this attack occurred in an affluent neighborhood in one of Florida's "safest cities?" Was it because a U.S. President, who had promised meaningful change, retreated after meeting privately with the NRA?[13] Or did Hollywood's celebrities spark action by donating to the March for Our Lives protest? Perhaps it was the raw passion of young adults standing up to a broken government, demanding action from elected officials.

Without a fully funded, publicly transparent, and comprehensive independent study on gun violence, determining which actions can save the most lives is challenging. Dave Cullen, author of *Parkland*, observed that the secret weapon of the March for Our Lives teens was their multi-front battle. They leveraged diverse voices, perspectives, and talents—healing each other while fighting for change.

Witnessing this vast youth-driven movement, I questioned my impact: "Who am I, compared to these giants? How can I make a positive difference? What will it take for us to be angry enough to make meaningful, enduring change so that school shootings never happen again?" The answer came when I realized my research skills as a librarian could gather fact-based data and uncover patterns to prevent future tragedies. My call to action is to simplify and make this information accessible, hoping it will save lives by fostering constructive dialogue and inspiring communities to take preventive action based on factual, nonpartisan data.

2

Good Trouble

During my time in the U.S. Air Force, my fellow airmen often joked, "Don't make Airman Aponte angry, because he'll write a letter!" Whenever I witnessed abuse of power or bullying, I felt compelled to speak up and escalate the issue through the chain of command. This drive landed me in "good trouble" a few times, as the late civil rights leader John Lewis might have called it. While not every outcome was positive, I've never regretted standing up for those who couldn't defend themselves or were too afraid to do so.

When my younger brother's Marine infantry unit deployed to Iraq and Afghanistan, I took action. I researched sustainable alternative fuels like algae, 80 MPG ultra-fuel-efficient vehicle patents under the 1993 *Partnership for a New Generation of Vehicles* (PNGV) "Supercar" project, and proposed a self-taxing strategy during periods of low oil prices to eliminate our dependence on foreign oil by investing in alternatives. In 2010, I compiled my findings into a 168-page spiral-bound "letter" to the President of the United States, which I also published as my first eBook and a short documentary film titled *Death of a Gas Guzzler*. While I was pleased to see the president implement some of my suggestions, I suspect it was more due to the administration's existing environmental agenda than my influence. In 1973, OPEC nations exposed our nation's vulnerability by being dependent on foreign sources of oil. It's disappointing that, despite the international conflicts affecting oil prices and resources post-September 11, 2001, we still have not fully developed sustainable alternatives to petroleum and other fossil fuels. This is the danger of not learning from history. Regardless, my goal was clear: I wanted to prevent more American families from sending their loved ones overseas to fight endless wars over finite petroleum resources.

My instinct to protect others likely stems from my martial arts upbringing and the abuse I endured as a child. I know the humiliation of being bullied in high school and the physical and verbal abuse from an intimidating stepfather. Some of the pain, fear, and helplessness I felt at five years old are still vivid. On one occasion, my stepfather, a military police officer, placed me on wooden beams inside a military barracks bathroom ceiling. Afraid of the height, I reluctantly dropped at his command, expecting him to catch me. Instead, I hit the bathroom sink as he laughed. Another time, he punched me so hard in the stomach that he carried me by the back of my clothing like a piece of luggage to a window so I could vomit outside. Crying was forbidden; he'd tell me to "suck it up, p***y!" At the dining table, his presence made me so fearful that I couldn't swallow my food. I would hyperventilate, trying to hold back tears. Training in martial arts as a teenager, I strengthened my abs and learned to kick hard and fast, ensuring I would never suffer that kind of pain or intimidation again.

When I was around the age of five, a police officer visited my classroom to talk about how police help people and the importance of adults not touching children inappropriately. He asked if any adult had touched us in harmful or inappropriate ways, and I raised my hand. Later, a white government sedan pulled up in front of our house while my mother was watching the soap opera *General Hospital* on T.V. I watched from the window, hoping they were there to take me away. The government representatives led us to the police station, where military police officers ripped me from my screaming mother's arms. They removed my shirt to photograph the bruises on my torso with a Polaroid camera before placing me in a foster home in California. The foster home owner was kind and even allowed me to choose my own cereal in the grocery store—a privilege I had never experienced before. I vividly remember picking *Boo-Berry* cereal, a blueberry-flavored cereal with marshmallows and a cartoon ghost character on the box. This simple yet trivial privilege of choosing something for myself filled me with so much gratitude. The other foster kids and I played tetherball in the backyard, enjoying a safe, violence-free environment. This was a safe place I had been missing as a child. Soon after this, my biological father learned of my situation and drove from New Mexico to California to rescue me.

I don't share these experiences for sympathy, but to illustrate my visceral understanding of the frustration, anger, and vicious cycle of bullying and child abuse. Without counseling and support, these traumatic events can fester, leading to destructive outcomes. As a result, I'm ashamed to admit that, in my youth, I was both the bullied and the bully. Many years later, I learned that my former stepfather had also been abused by his father—a cruel cycle doomed to repeat itself. It was only in the past decade that we made amends. Before he passed away from cancer, he often joined my family for holiday dinners, and our arguments were about politics and wild conspiracy theories fueled by social media misinformation. To those who have experienced this type of abuse, I say there is strength and light at the end of the tunnel when we learn to grow through the pain and forgive ourselves and others. Because of my instinct to protect others, I feel that staying silent after the Parkland mass shooting would make my hands just as blood-stained as those of the shooter. Never again.

3

Bookmarks in Life

As a child growing up as a military dependent—affectionately known as an "Army brat"—I can bookmark some of my favorite memories with the release of a popular movie or song. One of those cherished moments was watching my first movie in a theater with my father. Our family was stationed at White Sands Missile Range, a military base set against the desert landscape of New Mexico, bordering El Paso, Texas. The original *Ghostbusters* movie was playing as a Saturday matinee on base, with tickets costing only a dollar. My go-to movie snack was a three-foot red licorice rope. Few experiences rival the joy of watching a comedy in a theater packed with about 100 Army G.I.s, roaring with laughter at a Bill Murray and Dan Aykroyd classic film. Sadly, not all children have been able to share such joyous connections with their parents—like those tragically affected by the Aurora, Colorado movie theater mass shooting in 2012, where 12 lives were lost and 58 others injured during a showing of a *Batman* movie.[1]

The song *Livin' on a Prayer* by Bon Jovi whisks me back to fourth grade art class, where we created rock 'n' roll music videos using large, clunky VHS cameras. Yardstick rulers became pretend electric guitars, and wooden-handled paint brushes served as drumsticks. I begged my father to let me spike my hair into a neon-colored mohawk with Elmer's Glue, but he refused. Instead, I combed my hair out into an afro, embracing my naturally curly Puerto Rican hair—a look reminiscent of the late artist Bob Ross. Back then, the idea of classmates bringing guns to school was unthinkable. Yet, between 1990 and 2019, at least 46 accidental firearm discharges occurred in schools, injuring and killing shooters' friends, classmates, and even themselves.

Hold On to the Night by Richard Marx takes me back to a crisp fall day in Vicenza, Italy, when I hit the winning home run in a baseball game. Our family was stationed at a U.S. Army base, and that evening I attended my middle school homecoming dance, with *Hold On to the Night* as the theme song. Yet, I was too nervous to ask Courtney—a girl with long, wavy hair, green eyes, and freckles—to dance. My young heart broke as I watched her dance with my friend instead. These are the kinds of memories children should experience during their developmental years—treasured moments of innocence and growth—not the horrors of the Westside Middle School shooting in 1998, where five lives were lost and 10 others injured by two boys, aged 11 and 13.

I wish I had a popular song or movie to bookmark memories of my high school prom or an athletic triumph, but those rites of passage were eclipsed by the looming threat of gun violence. However, the most meaningful bookmark in my life came years later: *Thinking Out Loud* by Ed Sheeran marked the day I married the love of my life, Eileen, at Castle Otttis—a coastal, private castle in St. Augustine, Florida, the oldest city in the United States. As I write this, I find it ironic that my wife has long, wavy hair, green eyes, and freckles. This time, I didn't hesitate. I got the girl. At our wedding reception, we danced to *Thinking Out Loud*. Then, just as the song reached the final stanza, the speaker cut out. Without missing a beat, our family and friends carried us forward, singing the final lyrics aloud so we could finish our dance. Eileen has helped me overcome past fears about love and relationships, proving that some bookmarks in life hold not just memories, but profound lessons.

When I read the sobering book *#NeverAgain*, by Parkland school shooting survivors David and Lauren Hogg, it pains me to see their lives bookmarked and impacted not by inspiring pop music or movies, but by the violence of the 1999 Columbine High School mass shooting; the terrorists attacks of September 11, 2001; the 2012 Sandy Hook Elementary School mass shooting; the 2013 Los Angeles International Airport shooting; and the 2018 Marjory Stoneman Douglas High School mass shooting. These events have produced more terror and violence than any child should ever have to endure, especially before they are even old enough to vote.

As a child, one of my biggest concerns at school was whether the person who wanted to fight me would do so one-on-one or bring along a group of his buddies—until I attended civilian public schools in Hawaii and Florida. Fights usually took place behind the school, far from the teachers' view. There were no weapons involved—just raw, amateur grappling, punches, and kicks. When the fight ended, it was truly over, and everyone walked away...alive. Ironically, some of my closest childhood friendships began after a fistfight. I can still recall a few of my favorite t-shirts being ripped during these unconventional introductions. While the idea of enemies turning into friends after a fight may seem illogical to some, teenagers often don't need a rational explanation for things to work out in the end. If only our elected representatives could follow suit—engaging in civilized debates and emerging with mutual respect to constructively tackle the challenges facing Americans and our allies. Instead, it appears they often choose to enact discriminatory laws that fail to address the everyday problems of their constituents.

When I attended Marjory Stoneman Douglas High School, the thought of bringing a gun to school never crossed my mind because there were always adults I assumed I could turn to if things got too intense. These adults included the school resource officer, the principal, teachers, and my parents. I also had the fear of God within me, as I was raised by a strict Puerto Rican father who served as a sergeant in the Army and was a devout Christian. My father's foundation of discipline was a triple whammy. I learned to appreciate this gift later in life because my divorced parents actually stayed actively involved in my life and did their best to raise me properly with a strong moral foundation.

Perhaps I was shielded from the world of gun violence, drugs, and gangs because we mostly lived on military bases. I think parents serving in the military may be stricter than civilian parents because the culture of discipline in the services is generally more ingrained. There is also greater accountability from military superiors. If a child causes problems at school and a parent is not dealing with the issue, then the parent's commanding officer may get involved. I still recall my father telling me about a single parent stationed overseas who was sent back to the mainland U.S. because her child was causing too many problems at school.

Today's parents are working harder than ever to meet financial obligations, leaving them with less time, energy, and support to help their children develop essential social and coping skills. This isn't an excuse for bad behavior; it's a reflection of a generation grappling with economic inflation and an overabundance of technology designed to distract rather than constructively engage. Despite their prevalence, cell phones, video games, and social media don't seem to improve social skills. A Pew Research Center study found that 54% of teens feel they spend too much time on their smartphones.[2] In response to the dangers of using smartphones and social media, I had the privilege to interview former resource officer and author of *Parenting in the Digital World*, Clayton Cranford, a.k.a. "The Cyber Safety Cop." He encourages internet safety for teens by asking parents to wait until their children are 16 before buying them a smartphone. If a child needs a phone at a younger age, Cranford suggests buying them a flip phone.

Online bullying is a harsh reality, with people often being more vicious online than in person. One of my in-laws, who is studying to become a Christian minister, frequently attacks those with differing political and religious views on X (formerly Twitter). A distant cousin of mine is an actual Christian preacher, who not only attacks others with different views and lifestyles on Facebook, but also criticizes other Christians who worship differently than he does. Victims of this type of harassment can only retaliate by responding to, blocking, or reporting the offending profiles, as there's little risk of physical or legal consequences. If these virtual bullies confronted someone in person so harshly, the response would likely be more direct.

My generation learned social skills in our youth through direct confrontation, often referred to as the "Trial by Knuckle Sandwich" method. It's no wonder today's young adults feel more anxiety, especially if they haven't learned to ignore hateful rhetoric, de-escalate conflict, and manage stress. Sometimes, it's healthier to unplug from electronics and take a walk in nature. Thanks to my goal of completing this book and *The Ultimate U.S. School Shooting Reference Guide, Volumes 1-3*, I often spend days or weeks without checking social media. I've removed all social media apps from my phone, except for Instagram to share cat videos with my wife, and LinkedIn for professional connections. I've also canceled my personal, author, and librarian accounts on X due to my negative user experiences and how the platform is currently managed. Just like any consumer product, you're voting with your time and money. In my view, this social media platform doesn't deserve either from me. Unplugging and boycotting such platforms has led to less stress and more fulfillment as I work toward positive goals for my community and myself.

What I enjoyed most about the book *#NeverAgain* is seeing these kids for who they really are: normal teenagers with normal experiences, thrown into an extraordinary situation. They rose to the occasion, met the challenge, and inspired an entire nation to march in support of making our schools safe havens to learn again. What alarmed me most is witnessing how these teens, who just survived a horrific mass shooting, were constantly attacked online by cyberbullies simply for exercising their First Amendment rights to speak out against gun violence and fight for school safety. Suspicious, faceless accounts and conspiracy talk show hosts spread hateful rhetoric and lies about the students being "crisis actors" for months after the Marjory Stoneman Douglas High School shooting. Some attacked 14-year-old Lauren Hogg online, posting, "You're going to hell, you're an actress, your whole family is going to hell."[3] A well-known conspiracy theorist radio show host devoted an entire segment to likening David Hogg and Emma González to Hitler.[4] Such behavior is disgraceful, cruel, and falls far below the dignity expected of Americans. The toxic mix of hatred, division, and pettiness has fractured our nation. The relentless attacks on these brave students highlight the urgent need for a more compassionate and respectful discourse in our society.

In Sun Tzu's ancient military strategy text, *The Art of War*, turning an enemy against itself is the most effective way to manipulate a superior adversary into destroying itself. It is of vital importance to consider which foreign and domestic adversaries would benefit the most from widespread political division in the United States. I implore you, do not give hatred and cyberbullies the dignity of a platform. We must all work together in order to make safety in schools a measurable reality instead of a manipulated statistic on paper. For everyone else who continues to illegally harass children, there are open-source intelligence tools and free apps (i.e. screen recorders) that can help identify, document, and report violators to law enforcement. These are the tools I currently use in order to report those who threaten gun violence toward others. You can screenshot comments, locate IP addresses, and report violent threats to local law enforcement. It is everyone's responsibility to help prevent gun violence and bullying. Getting into "good trouble" includes documenting and reporting any threats of violence to authorities.

I confess I am envious of how David and Lauren Hogg, as well as the other students of Marjory Stoneman Douglas High School, have been prepared for the real world. Today's students are taught to contemplate and debate social, moral, and political events in their classes. I know American adults, born and raised in the U.S., who do not know how many stars are on the American flag or the name of our national anthem, and even far less who are able to have an informed debate on existing bills in Congress. And yet, I am amazed by how many U.S. citizens claim to be experts on who should be naturalized based on religion and race factors alone. In *#NeverAgain*, 14-year old Lauren Hogg illustrated how she debated at least 35 Congressional bills during the 2017-2018 school year.[5] I don't recall having such an intellectually stimulating experience while attending Marjory Stoneman Douglas High School. To be fair, I was not a fan of high school in general because I was always the outsider who moved every three years as a military dependent. It was always a challenge to adapt to new cultures I was expected to assimilate into. The only classes at MSDHS that had a lasting impression on me were Spanish and Oceanography. However, the reasons for that lasting impression are not as scholarly as David's and Lauren's.

Initially, I did not want to include the following high school memory in this book until I read Andrew Pollack's revelation about Broward schools not documenting or disciplining bad behavior in his book *Why Meadow Died*. He suggested that troubled students are getting passed from one teacher to another with no paperwork trail to say, "This student needs help."[6] His research suggests that this failure is due to policies designed to help reduce the statistics that cause the school-to-prison pipeline (SPP). South Florida's *Sun Sentinel* newspaper reported that the culture of leniency allows children to engage in an endless loop of violations and second chances, creating a system where kids who commit the same offence for the tenth time may be treated like it's the first offence.[7] The report further reveals teachers and parents claiming that Broward schools are pressuring teachers not to send students to administration for punishment in order to avoid tarnishing the school's image.

I suspect this culture of leniency predates 2018 by several years. In my Spanish class at Marjory Stoneman Douglas High School, I can vividly recall two memories. I remember my Caucasian teacher, who had an impressive command of the Spanish language with a perfect

Hispanic accent and pronunciation. Secondly, I also remember a troublemaking classmate who was regularly trying to skip class. On one particular day, the teacher had enough of his antics when the student requested another hall pass to use the restroom. She denied his request. The student then proceeded to stand at the corner of the room, unzipped his pants, and urinated on the classroom floor. He was sent to the administrator's office, but I do not believe he was ever suspended from school for defacing school property and publicly exposing himself in a classroom filled with minors. I appreciate the effort to give young people a second chance in order to avoid a life in the prison system, but surely there are better solutions than ignoring or underreporting bad school behavior, violations, and crimes.

In my opinion, the students attending Marjory Stoneman Douglas today are infinitely more impressive and, hopefully, more informed than I was at their age. They give me hope for the future of this nation, assuming we are able to work together and distinguish the difference between credible news and divisive social media propaganda fueled by the power of artificial intelligence—especially during election cycles. Between classes, these kids are discussing engineering, politics, and black holes in space that can bend time...for fun. I don't remember talking about anything in high school more profound than pretty girls that were out of my league and the latest martial arts B-movie that had just come out on VHS...at Blockbuster Video. The young adults that launched March for Our Lives are much cooler and exponentially more ambitious in their academic studies than I could have ever hoped to be in my high school years.

The purpose of this book is to continue the work initiated by David and Lauren, leveraging patterns found in past school shootings at a level unmatched by any single resource, including the U.S. government and major news outlets. The results of nearly four years of research are compiled in my other books, *The Ultimate U.S. School Shooting Reference Guide, Volumes 1-3*. This is significant because, to my knowledge as a librarian, a comprehensive, pattern-seeking database of gun violence in schools has never been published in the United States. In my opinion, this political failure should be diagnosed as mental insanity and no longer tolerated by voters. A close exception is the *Gun Violence Archive*, which has done an outstanding job tracking gun violence and providing customizable search options. *Everytown for Gun Safety* is another exceptional nonprofit organization that has summarized gun violence statistics effectively in its research. The goal of my four books on school shootings is to improve upon and expand this research, making it easily digestible for parents and the general public.

In contrast to any predictable and misleading attacks I am prepared to receive for writing this book and *The Ultimate U.S. School Shooting Reference Guide, Volumes 1-3*, it is important to note that I earned the Small Arms Expert Marksmanship ribbon with an M-16 rifle in the U.S. Air Force. My younger brother served in Iraq and Afghanistan as an infantryman in the U.S. Marine Corps and as a police officer in North Carolina. My best friend was a prison guard for the Sheriff Department in Colorado. My father served in the U.S. Army for 20 years and is qualified with the M-16 rifle, M-60 machine gun, M72 LAW Anti-Tank Weapon, M79 Grenade Launcher, and a two and a half-ton truck with a .50 caliber machine gun. I illustrate these points because I understand and respect there is a purpose and place for responsible gun ownership in this country. Please do not lean on the crutch and convenience of political assumptions before giving this book and *The Ultimate U.S. School Shooting Reference Guide, Volumes 1-3* a chance to present their case. We do not have time to be bothered with the petty differences of politics, race, religion, and social status. Now is the time to recognize fact from fiction. Now is the time to work together. Our survival literally depends on it.

My research reveals patterns in school shootings in order to find real solutions that can help prevent them from happening in the future. This information should appeal to all parents, students, educators, law enforcement officers, researchers, and journalists, as well as extended family members of school-aged children, regardless of political affiliation. Whether or not you have children of your own, if you are a warm-blooded, empathetic person who cares about the safety of children, this information should deeply resonate with you. As David and Lauren Hogg reveal in their book, *#NeverAgain*, "none of us can do this alone and we need you."[8] Our future generations deserve safe learning environments that do not make them feel they are in a prison filled with teachers carrying handguns. My generation never resorted to such extremes, and neither did our parents' or grandparents' generations. This is the United States of America. We can, and must, do better.

4

Superhero Parents Emerge From Gun Violence

Lori Alhadeff and Kirk Smalley.
Images courtesy of Lori Alhadeff and Kirk Smalley.

One could argue that raising a child can be counted among the greatest and most underestimated acts of heroism. Why? It is a courageous act whereby you are providing a lifetime of love, hope, protection and guidance for your children.

But what happens when a parent suffers the loss of a child due to a preventable tragedy, such as gun violence? It is then that parents must really dig deep and find their strength. The result? Heroes walking among us.

The capes worn by devoted parents are invisible but mighty. They are the day guardians and night watchmen who ignite hope, offer protection, and whisper sweet adoration into the ears of their little ones. Offering solace through each frightening nightmare and every bruised "owie," parents inspire resilience in their children and instill in them the courage to face even the most violent of life's storms.

So what is the greatest threat to raising a child? Books dealing with borderline subjects? Violent video games, movies, or music? You might think so, right? However, according to the Associated Press and Northeastern University, guns—surpassing even car accidents—was the leading cause of death for children and teenagers in 2020. "We are a nation of gun violence survivors and tragically, our ranks continue to grow," said Sarah Burd-Sharps, Senior Director of Research at Everytown for Gun Safety. "No parent wants to believe that gun violence could ever invade their community, but the unrelenting reality of our gun violence epidemic in America is that each day, parents across the country are being proven wrong." And when these parents are proven wrong—faced with the unspeakable reality of gun violence in their backyards—it is within the very ruins of grief that innocence is lost and certain parents emerge as unsung heroes. Their invisible capes are "woven" from resilience, not fabric. Their superpowers—indestructible as iron—are forged in the inferno of anguish. With each step, they tread the tightrope between sorrow and purpose, channeling their heartache into a shield for other children. Activism becomes their battle cry, a defiant stand to prevent the relentless tide of tragedy from repeating itself again and again.

Lori Alhadeff lost her 14-year-old daughter, Alyssa, in the 2018 Marjory Stoneman Douglas High School mass shooting in Parkland, Florida. "She (Alyssa) never met a person she couldn't make laugh. Her laugh was contagious to everyone that heard her within a mile radius," according to *The Eagle Eye* student newspaper 2018 special edition memoriam, published in honor of the victims of the mass shooting. In the unprovoked attack, 17 students and teachers were killed, and 17 others were injured, with a legally purchased AR-15-style rifle. Since then, Lori has focused her pain into a positive platform for change by creating the nonprofit organization "Make Our Schools Safe".

She has tirelessly fought and won bipartisan support of "Alyssa's Law" in New Jersey, Florida, New York, Tennessee, Texas, Utah, and Oklahoma, while successfully introducing the law in several other states. This critical piece of legislation addresses the issue of law enforcement response time when a life-threatening emergency occurs, shortening it dramatically by installing a panic button in school classrooms.

Lori's strength and commitment to find bi-partisan support in order to help keep kids safe in schools is inspiring. Her efforts are gaining attention and making a true impact, clearly, as she and at least two other parents of the Parkland school shooting victims were invited to the White House for the passing of President Biden's "Bipartisan Safer Communities Act."

In my first podcast interview in 2022, I asked Lori how she remains strong and focused while accomplishing so much to protect other children. She admitted that her strength still comes from her daughter, Alyssa. She explained that she has made it her mission to be Alyssa's voice, determined not to let her beloved daughter's death be in vain. Instead, Lori channels her energy into continuing Alyssa's fight.

There is even more fueling Lori's determination. Ensuring that Alyssa's brothers, their friends, and all children are safe in school is deeply personal for her. The unwavering love and support she receives from her family and friends empower her to keep pushing for change in her community and beyond.

The family has also welcomed a Goldendoodle therapy dog named Roxie. Lori shared how Roxie's loving nature has helped them navigate some of the hardest moments of their grieving journey. She believes Alyssa would approve of Roxie and everything her mother is doing in her name. "Alyssa was such a fighter and had a big voice. She was the captain of her soccer team. I know Alyssa would want me to keep going and keep fighting for her," Lori said.   For most parents, losing a child is a death sentence to the soul; kryptonite to the spirit. After all, it is an understood expectation that the natural way of things is for children to carry on the memories of their mothers and fathers, not the other way around. But for some parents, losing a child in such a preventable tragedy is an unwelcome baptism by fire where their heroism is tested. After being slowly saturated by endless tears, a defiant force sometimes emerges from the now-tamed flames. This force can be recognized as a supernatural power of purpose and destiny.

In 2022, I had the sobering and humbling privilege of speaking with Kirk Smalley, whose 11-year old son, Ty, committed suicide with a gun after being relentlessly bullied in school for two years. Kirk's wife, Laura, worked in their son's school and had raised concerns about the bullying, only to have the administrators dismiss her concerns saying, "Boys will be boys." The school principal actually told her, "He (Ty) just needs to toughen up, cupcake."

When Kirk's son was pushed to the point of retaliation against a bully one day, he was suspended. That day, when his parents returned home from work, they found not that their son had done his homework or chores, but instead, that he had taken his own life. Since that day, Kirk has done extensive research and learned that we are losing kids on a daily basis to suicide directly related to bullying.

Furthermore, Kirk now has a list of over 66,000 children we have lost in America within the last 8 years alone. The youngest one on the list is only 6 years old. Kirk is now the president of the nonprofit organization, Stand for the Silent, which is committed to changing kids' lives and bringing awareness about bullying and the real devastation it causes.

In 2020, Kirk suffered yet another heartbreaking loss as his wife passed away. Kirk shares how this grief has only served to strengthen his desire to make a difference, saying, "I gotta be the best man I can possibly be, and I gotta save as many babies as I can while I'm still here."

I asked Kirk how he finds strength after these tragic experiences. He explains, "I get messages, literally by the thousands, from kids that I have spoken to. We've talked to 3,991 schools now; a little over 3.5 million kids. I get messages from most kids that we've talked to literally by the thousands, saying, 'You saved my life. I was going to kill myself until I heard what you had to say, and now I'm not. And I want to help you make it stop, Mr. Smalley.'"

Kirk and Laura Smalley traveled to over 6,025 schools and spoke with over 4.15 million students. On March 10, 2011, Kirk and Laura met privately with President Obama and First Lady Michelle Obama in the White House prior to attending the first ever White House conference on bullying.

Each of these extraordinary examples showcases parents who have demonstrated superhero strength and fortitude following unimaginable grief. The ability to summon such Herculean power of will and spirit to help save the lives of other children after losing one's own child is unfathomable, and deeply commendable.

These parents have inspired thousands of others to commit to serving in their local communities by taking action against gun violence. They have proven that we are powerful when we focus on shared goals and work together to achieve them. Superheroes like these parents do not rely on "thoughts and prayers." Instead, they expect—and demand—meaningful change. More than anyone, these superhero parents recognize that the fates of generations of children to come desperately hang on the collective power of love, hope, protection and guidance from a collectively committed community.

5

Everyone in the Community Has a Role

Preventing students from bringing weapons onto school property begins at home. Parents play a vital role in safeguarding their children from the risks associated with illegal access to firearms. Among boys aged 14 to 17 featured in *The Ultimate School Shooting Reference Guide, Volumes 1-3*, this issue is particularly alarming, as many in this age group are most likely to use an illegally obtained handgun to resolve conflicts. To address this, parents must remain actively involved in their children's lives—getting to know their closest friends and monitoring their electronic devices, journals, and online activity. To make this task more manageable, major cellphone and internet providers offer parental control technologies and helpful tips.

However, for single-parent families, this level of supervision can be especially challenging. Drawing from personal experience, I understand these struggles intimately. My single mother—a gun owner—who raised four children on welfare, balanced a full-time job, community college, and the challenge of communicating in a second language. Her no-nonsense approach, paired with the foundation of discipline my military father instilled during my early years, ensured we stayed on the right path. In addition, martial arts became a vital anchor for our family as we trained together. Through the five tenets of Taekwondo—courtesy, integrity, perseverance, self-control, and indomitable spirit—we developed a set of core principles that kept us grounded. These values were so deeply ingrained that the idea of bringing a firearm to school never even occurred to us.

In single-parent households, the eldest siblings often assume significant responsibilities, such as ensuring their younger siblings are fed, safe, and focused on homework while the parent juggles multiple jobs. Even in two-parent homes, the rising cost of living often means both parents are working long hours, leaving children unsupervised for extended periods. This is where the broader community becomes an essential safeguard. Trusted family members, friends, religious leaders, athletic coaches, martial arts instructors, neighbors, teachers, and principals can all contribute meaningfully to fill these gaps and provide the support that children need to stay safe.

Responsible gun owners have a personal duty to secure their firearms against theft—especially theft by their own children. Unfortunately, irresponsible gun owners are unlikely to read this book or follow any reasonable advice to protect children. My research revealed that in at least 482 school shooting cases, the firearms used were obtained illegally, often directly from the home. Stashing a gun in an unlocked glove compartment, under a pillow, in a sock drawer, a purse pocket, or on top of the refrigerator is not securing it. True security means storing firearms in a gun safe that prevents children's access.

Schools alone cannot shoulder the burden of keeping firearms off their premises. While millions of dollars can be spent on security measures, no amount of funding can replace the simple yet vital practices of responsible gun ownership. Properly storing firearms in locked safes, teaching children about gun safety, and routinely ensuring weapons are secure are essential steps that every gun owner must take. These actions are not just preventative—they are lifesaving.

The urgency of these measures becomes painfully clear when considering the tragedy at Marjory Stoneman Douglas High School in

Parkland, Florida. In just six and a half minutes, the shooter claimed 17 lives and left 17 others injured, forever altering countless families and a community. While some survivors and victims' families have transformed their grief into powerful activism, others quietly bear the weight of trauma—exhausted by public attention and seeking healing, purpose, and a way forward. Protecting children in schools demands a comprehensive approach: armed and trained resource officers, security guards stationed in parking lots, metal detectors, controlled entry points, emotional intelligence coaching, and trusted networks of students who can provide critical intelligence. Schools must be adequately funded and equipped to respond swiftly and decisively to active threats, because when lives are at stake, every second matters.

Yet, the true heroes in this fight are often overlooked. Officers, teachers, and coaches play an indispensable role in creating safe learning environments. Students, too, are a powerful resource in preventing violence. By training school staff to build stronger bonds of trust with students, we can create a foundation of safety where children feel comfortable speaking up. This trust can save lives. Teachers and resource officers must also be empowered to enforce discipline and uphold laws on school property, regardless of public optics. Leniency policies that ignore or underreport crimes send a dangerous message: that disruptive and illegal behavior carries no consequences. Such policies endanger everyone—students, teachers, and even the perpetrators themselves.

The most critical resource in preventing school shootings, however, is the students themselves. Every threat—whether of violence or suicide—must be taken seriously, even if it comes from a friend or family member. In at least 71 incidents of school gun violence, the shooter verbally notified one or more people before the shooting. Reports reveal that their friends stayed silent because they didn't take the threat seriously. Speaking up can save lives, including the life of the person making the threat. I witnessed this firsthand when my closest friend confided in me about his suicidal thoughts after separating from his wife. For months, his family and I looked after him, demanded that his firearms be locked away, and encouraged him to seek professional counseling. Today, he is in a healthier mental state, with goals and hope for the future. His brother still holds his firearms in a locked safe—a precaution that undoubtedly saved his life.

This lesson is echoed in countless tragedies. In one case, 17-year-old Jamie Rouse told five friends about his plan to carry out a shooting at Richland High School in 1995. One friend even drove him to school on the morning of the attack, knowing Rouse had a gun. "I guess I wanted someone to stop me," Rouse later admitted.[1] These chilling words underscore a vital truth: when someone shares a threat, they may be asking for help. Taking every threat seriously and speaking up can prevent unimaginable loss. It is a message that cannot be repeated enough—speaking up saves lives.

6

Understanding School Gun Violence

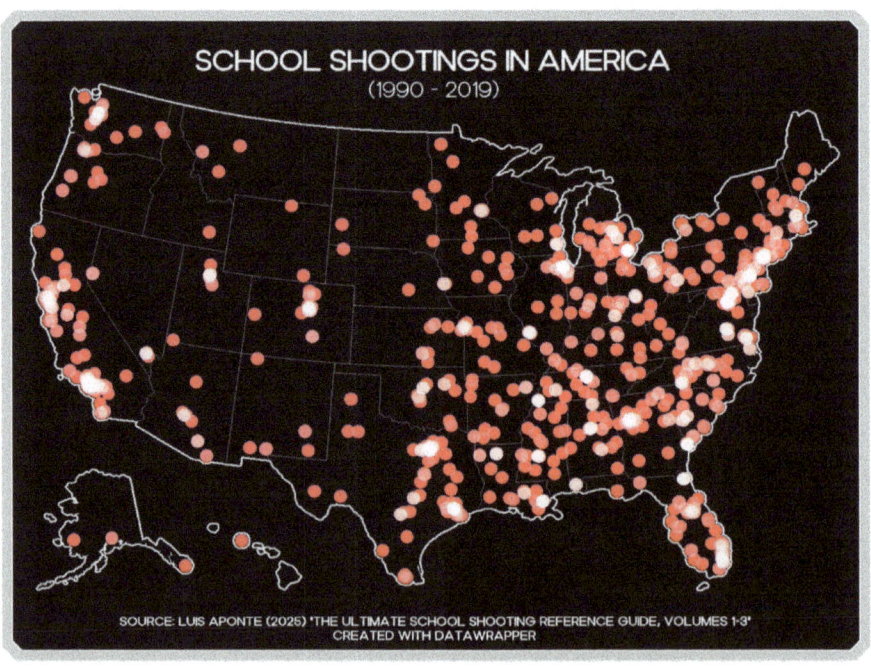

Heatmap of U.S. School Shootings (1990-2019)
Created by Michelle Quigley. Based on "The Ultimate U.S. School Shooting Reference Guide, Volumes 1-3" by Luis D. Aponte, MLIS

When I began this journey to find solutions that could help save lives in schools, I had no idea how big this project would become. Reading true crime reports from 1,204 incidents of school gun violence weighed heavily on my mental health, especially after reading stories that involved children in grade school and kindergarten. Between 1990 and 2019, at least 59 victims were 10 years old or younger. Sometimes, I needed days and, sometimes, weeks away from my research to recover from the disturbing stories. Occasionally, I would break down in tears out of empathy for the grieving families. In those moments, I would hold my wife in silence, overwhelmed with gratitude for the gift she has been in my life. Throughout that period, I estimate we took at least 360 walks at the Okeeheelee Nature Center, a local nature park in West Palm Beach, Florida. We would go "forest bathing"—a term used by the Japanese meaning to immerse oneself in nature through the senses in order to de-stress and improve one's well-being. In the process, we discovered many favorite hiding spots of local rabbits, tortoises, and owls. These walks helped alleviate the emotional toll of conducting this type of research.

Whenever I considered giving up on completing this book and *The Ultimate U.S. School Shooting Reference Guide, Volumes 1-3*, I would reflect on the victims of the Marjory Stoneman Douglas High School mass shooting in 2018. Their families and friends continue to endure immense suffering, and they deserve fact-based solutions to prevent such a tragedy from recurring. As a form of art therapy and an effort to honor their memories, I began painting portraits of some of the victims, despite lacking formal training. I simply projected their images onto a canvas and then painted their portraits with different shades of black and white acrylic paint. This private endeavor motivated me to persist in my work and ensure that their legacies endure, even though they will never have the chance to fully experience all the joys and nuances of life. Due to my inexperience, each portrait took about 10-14 hours to complete.

Helena Ramsay, Age 17.
Portrait Painted by Luis D. Aponte

Aaron Louis Feis, Age 37.
Portrait Painted by Luis D. Aponte.

Martin Duque Anguiano, Age 14.
Portrait Painted by Luis D. Aponte.

Joaquin Oliver, Age 17.
Portrait Painted by Luis D. Aponte.

Alaina Joann Petty, Age 14.
Portrait Painted by Luis D. Aponte.

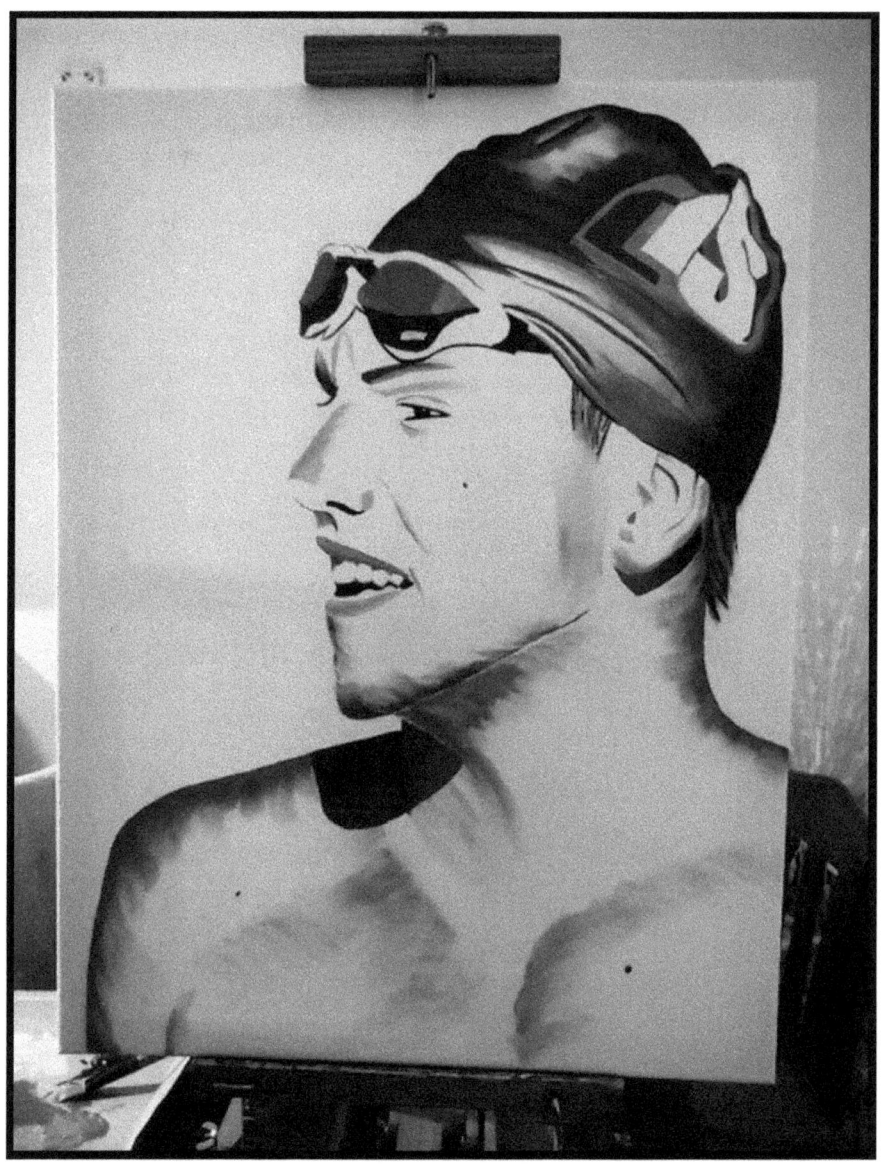

Nicholas Paul Dworet, Age 17.
Portrait Painted by Luis D. Aponte.

Jaime Taylor Guttenberg, Age 14.
Portrait Painted by Luis D. Aponte.

Meadow Jade Pollack, Age 18.
Portrait Painted by Luis D. Aponte.

Alyssa Alhadeff, Age 14.
Portrait Painted by Luis D. Aponte.

Some of these portraits went through two or three revisions, as my initial attempts fell short of my expectations. After more than 100 hours of self-directed art therapy, I returned my focus to completing my research into U.S. school shooting patterns. Parents, teachers, and students deserve straightforward answers and effective legal tools to protect themselves—rather than depending on the frequently insufficient actions of elected officials.

The starting point of my research began with nonprofit organizations dedicated to studying gun violence, such as:
- The Gun Violence Archive
- Everytown for Gun Safety
- The Naval Postgraduate School Center for Homeland Defense and Security
- Ballotpedia

Several news outlets have cited these organizations in the past. Indeed, these are great organizations that did gather some of the most abundant public sources of school shooting incidents at the time of their publication. However, I felt that more information was needed, and that it would be a mistake to only rely on the same resources as every other media outlet without doing my own due diligence. This determination led me to continue my research by reviewing school gun violence reports from the FBI, U.S. Secret Service, U.S. Department of Education, and the U.S. Government Accountability Office. Due to the different ways in which each of these institutions defined a school shooting, I was surprised and disappointed to learn of the stark contrast in their results, and in the severe underrepresentation of the national crisis of school gun violence in America.

Inconsistent Definitions of a "School Shooting"

Here are a few examples of the contrasting ways in which different U.S. government institutions define, and therefore evaluate, school shootings. I have taken this passage straight from an article I wrote and published, "Reviewing and Updating the Documented Historical Reports on School Shootings: New Strategies to Help Save Lives on Campuses." This article was featured in *Education*, a peer-reviewed education journal on December 15, 2022. With your indulgence, I feel this it is critical for you, the reader, to be aware of this conflicting and confusing information.

Federal Bureau of Investigation (FBI)

The 2019 FBI report, *Active Shooter Incidents in the United States from 2000-2018*,[1] focused only on active shooter events. The list includes gun violence incidents at elementary, middle, and high schools, as well as colleges and universities, and defines an active shooter as "an individual actively engaged in killing or attempting to kill people in a populated area."[2] Applying this definition, the FBI featured only 57 incidents in its analysis of school shootings that occurred between 2000-2018.[3]

U.S. Secret Service (USSS) and U.S. Department of Education (ED)

Alternatively, the *Safe School Initiative Report* submitted by the U.S. Secret Service and the U.S. Department of Education in 2004 focused only on targeted school violence, which they defined "as any incident of violence where a known or knowable attacker selects a particular target prior to their violent attack."[4] Further still, only 37 incidents of targeted school shootings and school attacks from December 1974 through May 2000 were analyzed in this report.[5]

U.S. Government Accountability Office (GAO)

The United States Government Accountability Office also published a report for Congressional Requesters entitled *K-12 Education Characteristics of School Shootings*.[6] However, their evaluation only focused on instances where students or staff were at risk in K-12 schools. They defined a school shooting as "any time a gun is fired on school grounds, on a bus, during a school event, during school hours, or right before or after school.7 Applying this definition, the U.S. GAO noted 318 incidents of school shootings for the school years 2009 through 2019.

Reevaluation Method Needed for Government Results

Applying the standards set forth by these three different government entities, I sought to independently research every school shooting reported between January 1, 1990 and January 1, 2020, a 30-year period, using library Boolean operators to help broaden and narrow the searches in library catalogs, Newspapers.com and NewsBank databases, and other internet sources. This process included using a combination of keyword search terms that may or may not have been used in previous studies, e.g., bullet, campus, college, discharge, discharged, elementary, firearm, gun, gunman, injured, killed, killer, killing, kills, murder, murderer, rifle, school, shoot, shooting, shootings, shoots, shot, slaying, suicide, and university. Thus, updated information was discovered and is noted here:

Updated FBI Results

Based on the FBI standard definition of active shooter events, I found approximately 119 incidents of school shootings for this same 30-year time period.

Updated USSS and ED Results

Based on the U.S. Secret Service and the U.S. Department of Education standard definition of targeted school violence, I found at least 397 incidents of school shootings during that same 30-year time period.

Updated GAO Results

Based on the United States Government Accountability Office's standard definition of school shooting events where students or staff were at risk and included only K-12 schools during school hours, or right before or after school, I found 821 incidents of school shootings for this same 30-year time period.

Thus, it is clear that exactly how the term "school shooting" is defined significantly impacts the effectiveness, scope, and public perception of the overall problem of gun violence in schools. Even within the narrow definitions set forth by the government organizations mentioned above, the use of library Boolean search terms still offered significantly larger comparative results:

- **FBI** – Before: 57 / After: 199 / Difference: 249%
- **USSS & ED** - Before: 37 / After: 397 / Difference: 972%
- **GAO**: Before: 318 / After: 821 / Difference: 158%

In order to effectively empower communities and law enforcement with information that will help develop customized solutions to disrupt the patterns that actually lead to school gun violence, a more inclusive and universal definition of school shootings must be consistently adopted across all U.S. government institutions.

To obtain a more encompassing and comprehensive representation of gun violence in schools with a significant sample size, I offer a complete definition of a school shooting as being any shooting from a firearm that occurred on or toward any school property; a school extracurricular activity; and/or school-sponsored event at any time of the day, night, or year when at least one person was killed or injured. A "school" is defined as any academic institution, including but not limited to, pre-kindergarten, elementary, middle, and high schools. It also includes colleges, universities, trade schools, and specialty schools (e.g., firearm training and missionary schools). The term, "school property" further includes school-owned or leased buildings, parking lots, bus stops, dormitories, athletic fields and courts, as well as the interior of school busses. Shootings on college campuses are also suggested for inclusion due to the ongoing presence of students and staff in dormitories, libraries, on campus grounds, at athletic and extracurricular events, etc.

Alternatively, I define a mass shooting in this book as an incident in which at least four individuals are shot, either injured or killed, including any alleged shooter(s) who may also have been shot during or immediately after the incident. This is different from the definition of a mass killing, which only focuses on the number of fatalities. While some organizations exclude the alleged shooter(s) from mass shooting results, I believe that including all individuals affected by the shooting provides communities and researchers a more accurate portrayal of the overall impact of gun violence in the United States.

Finally, I used two excellent paid news databases—Newspapers.com and NewsBank—to research and cross reference any results with police reports and court documents that may have been missed by both nonprofit organizations and government agencies.

From these statistics, we can draw several inferences related to school shootings in the United States. For example, the frequency or deadliness of school shooting incidents do not seem strictly tied to either strict or relaxed gun laws. States with both strict and relaxed gun laws experience such incidents, indicating that other factors contribute to this challenge. The number of school shootings have increased over the years under both Democratic and Republican U.S. president administrations. Major cities with dense populations are more susceptible to higher numbers of school shootings, regardless of their political affiliation. Surprisingly, the most dangerous school shootings have not been limited to large urban centers.

7

30 Years of School Shooting Trends

"What will stop the next school shooting?" This poignant question was asked by the grieving mother of a Parkland shooting victim. At the time, I didn't have fact-based answers for her, but I had painted a portrait of her daughter and gifted it to her family as a promise that she would never be forgotten. No parent, student, or teacher should ever have to endure such a tragedy. As an alumnus of Marjory Stoneman Douglas High School, I am deeply connected to this cause. In my efforts to prevent future tragedies, I analyzed patterns in 1,204 incidents of U.S. school gun violence. Here's what I uncovered:

In 1990, digitized newspapers and online news articles reported at least 19 school shootings in the United States. By 2019, that number had soared to 94—a staggering 494% increase. Remarkably, some of the deadliest school shootings in U.S. history coincided with a broader surge in school shootings and victims during the same years.

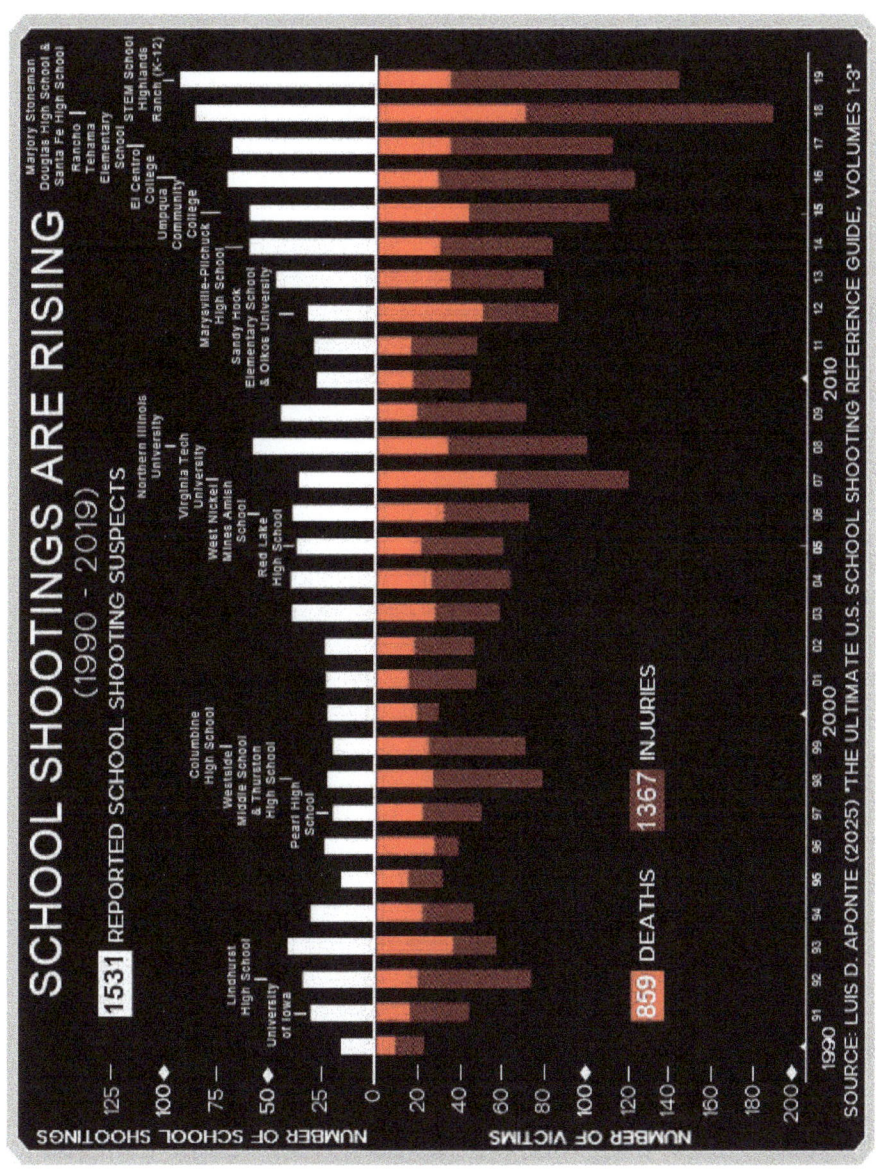

School shootings are rising (1990-2019).
Infographic created by Harrison Snell and Luis D. Aponte. Based on "The Ultimate U.S. School Shooting Reference Guide, Volumes 1-3" by Luis D. Aponte.

Handguns are the most frequently used firearms in school shootings, accounting for 76.5% of identified weapons. Their compact size allows them to be easily concealed in backpacks or clothing, often allowing them to go undetected due to inconsistent use of metal detectors and inadequate monitoring of access points. The most common types of handguns involved in school shootings are 9mm, .22-, and .38-caliber firearms.

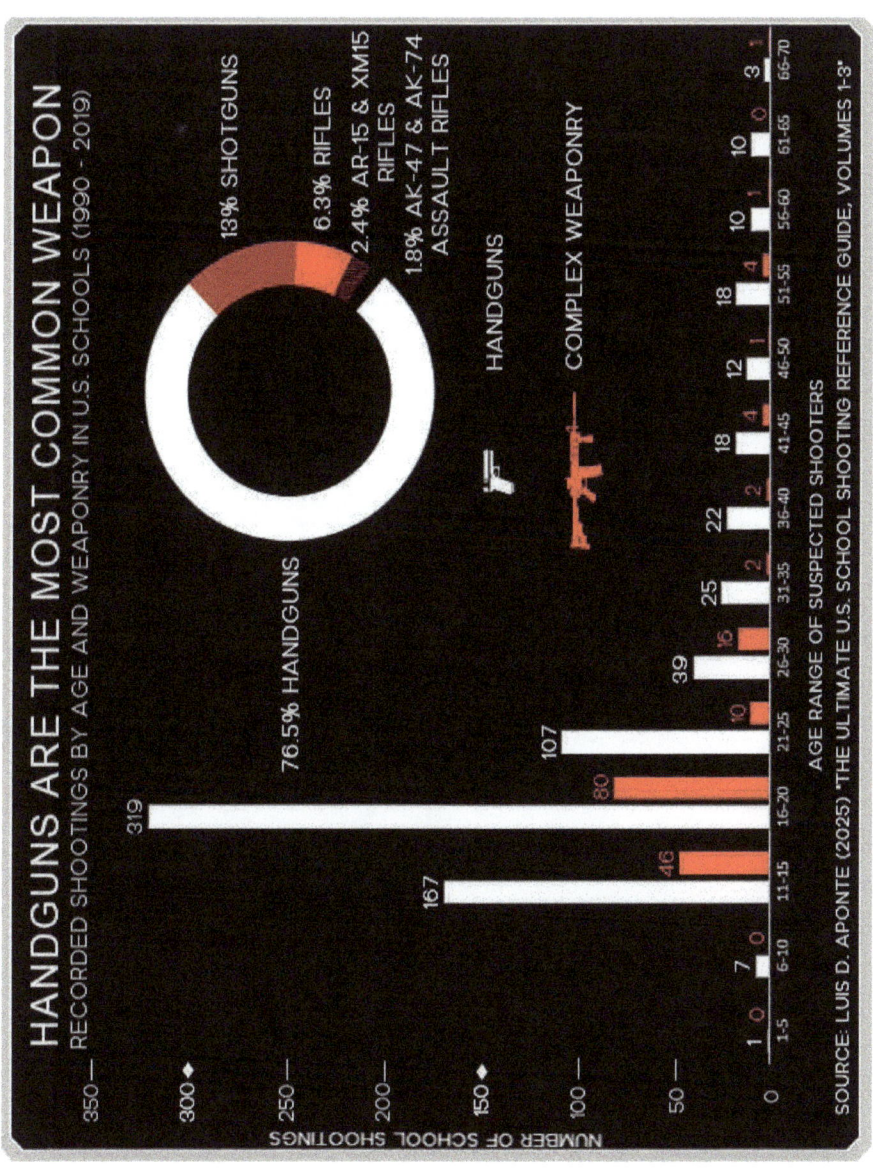

Handguns are the most common weapon in U.S. school shootings.

Infographic created by Harrison Snell and Luis D. Aponte. Based on "The Ultimate U.S. School Shooting Reference Guide, Volumes 1-3" by Luis D. Aponte.

Among males aged 13 to 17, illegal access to handguns is a significant threat. Once boys reach age 13, they are most likely to use an illegally obtained handgun to resolve conflicts. This suggests that addressing illegal underage access to firearms is critical for preventing future school shootings. Most incidents result in fewer than three deaths and often do not receive sufficient attention to drive prevention efforts, with many dismissed as being "isolated events." Consequently, parents may not fully grasp the extent of how guns enter schools. While mass shootings like Sandy Hook, Parkland, and Virginia Tech are harder to predict, there are often warning signs.

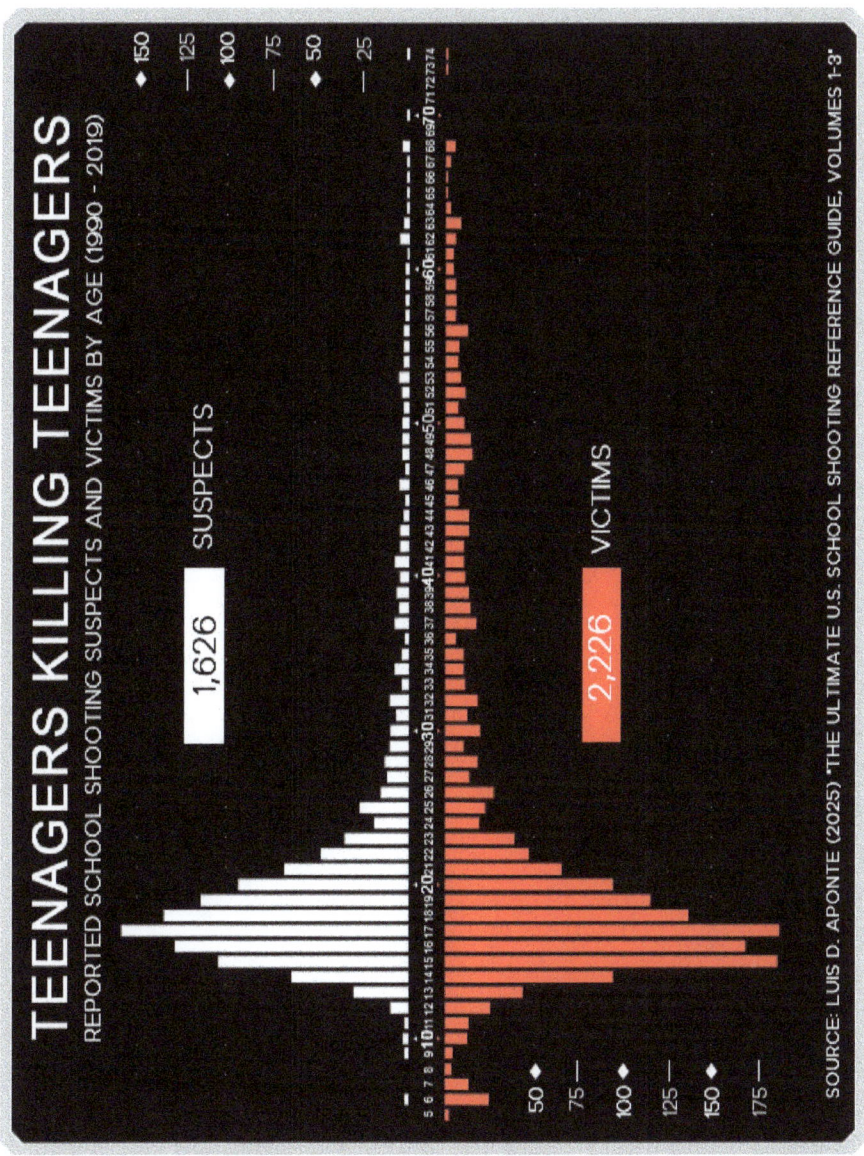

Teenagers killing teenagers. Reported school shooting suspects and victims by age (1990-2019).

Infographic created by Harrison Snell and Luis D. Aponte. Based on "The Ultimate U.S. Shooting Reference Guide, Volumes 1-3" by Luis D. Aponte.

Contrary to popular belief, mental illness, depression, and bullying do not rank among the top six factors triggering school shootings. Instead, the leading motivations are arguments and feuds, followed by accidents and gang-related activity. This suggests that preventing school shootings, and possibly violence in general, requires teaching critical social skills, such as conflict resolution and emotional mastery, before children reach age 13. Community-based mentoring programs could play a vital role in this effort.

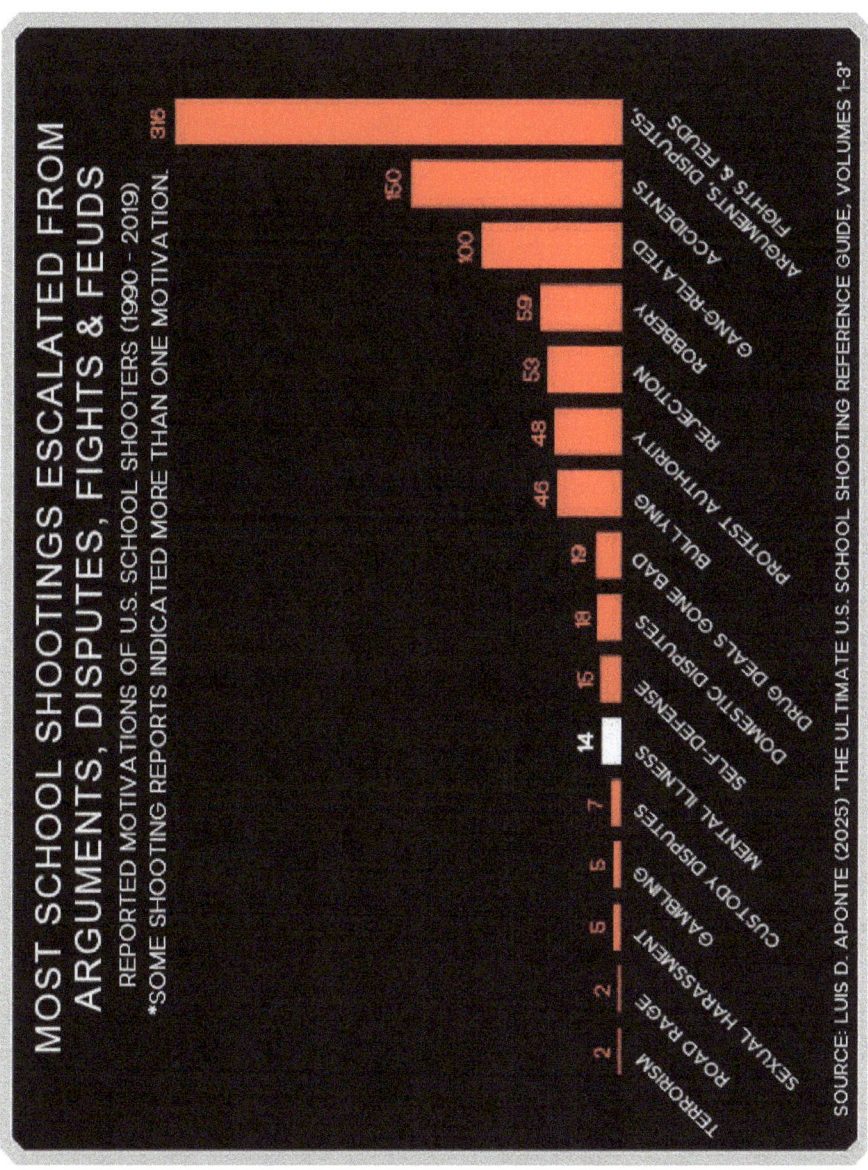

Most shootings escalated from fights and arguments. Reported motivations of U.S. school shooters (1990-2019).

Infographic created by Harrison Snell and Luis D. Aponte. Based on "The Ultimate U.S. School Shooting Reference Guide, Volumes 1-3" by Luis D. Aponte.

The inconsistent definition and research around school shootings has created a confusing public understanding of gun violence on school properties. A more comprehensive definition should include any shooting occurring on or toward school property, during extracurricular activities, or at school-sponsored events, regardless of the time of day or year it occurs, as long as at least one person is injured or killed.

School shootings occur in states with both strict and loose gun laws, indicating that legislative measures alone are not enough. Parents often ask, "What will stop the next school shooting?" The answer may lie in communities teaching young people vital life skills, like emotional mastery, conflict resolution, and gun safety, while also eliminating underage access to firearms. Although there is no one-size-fits-all solution, each community must conduct a nuanced analysis to understand and address the underlying causes.

Preventing the next school shooting may not receive the same recognition as engaging an active shooter, but saving even a single child's life is its own greatest reward.

8

Roots and Myths Behind Motivations

School shootings devastate communities, leaving behind not only grief but also a social media storm of unfounded assumptions and misplaced blame. Common scapegoats—illegal immigration, violent video games, radical ideologies, or mental illness—often dominate public discussions. Yet, an analysis of 1,204 school shootings between 1990 and 2019 reveals a far more complex and sobering reality. Contrary to popular belief, the majority of school shooters do not fall into these categories.

Instead, fights and disputes, not mental illness, drive most incidents of school gun violence. A staggering 26.2% of these tragedies are rooted in escalated arguments, personal feuds, and physical confrontations. Disputes over romantic relationships, stolen belongings, gang rivalries, or retaliation for past slights can ignite a deadly chain of events. In stark contrast, only 1.2% of school shootings are linked to diagnosed mental illness, based on publicly available reports. This mismatch between perception and reality underscores a crucial yet overlooked driver of violence: unresolved conflict.

To address these tragedies, we must confront a vital gap in prevention: teaching children and adults how to manage conflict and emotions effectively. The consequences of unresolved disputes are painfully real. Take the case of William B. Holmes III, a 19-year-old who allegedly shot five Duquesne University basketball players after a school dance in 2006, reportedly over an argument involving a girl.[1] Had William been equipped with conflict resolution skills and emotional mastery, this tragic event might have been avoided. Similarly, Dalton Lee Stidham, a 21-year-old who allegedly killed his ex-girlfriend, her uncle, and her cousin during a custody exchange for their 2-year-old son in 2013, might have found a constructive and honorable way to address his frustration.[2][3] Instead, his son is left to grow up without either parent. These heartbreaking examples highlight the urgent need to learn how to deescalate tensions before they spiral into violence. Imagine a generation empowered with the tools to negotiate, empathize, and reconcile differences instead of resorting to aggression. By fostering these skills early, we can defuse the powder kegs of tension before they explode.

Equally important is breaking the stigma around mental health. While not the predominant factor in school shootings, mental health challenges still warrant attention. Schools must lead the way in championing awareness initiatives, creating environments where students feel supported and safe to seek help. No one should struggle alone. By addressing both conflict and mental health proactively, we can reshape our approach to violence prevention, building safer spaces for every student to thrive.

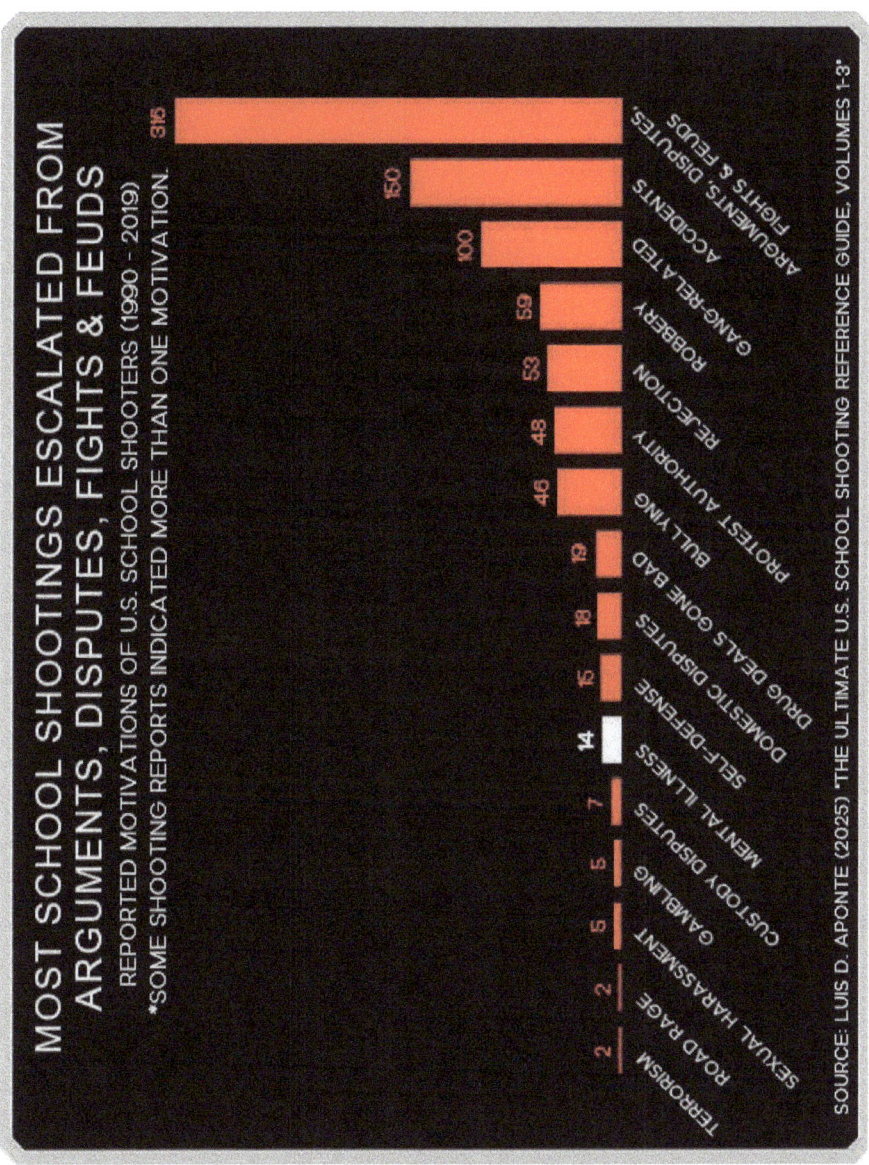

Most shootings escalated from fights and arguments. Reported motivations of U.S. school shooters (1990-2019).

Infographic created by Harrison Snell and Luis D. Aponte. Based on "The Ultimate U.S. School Shooting Reference Guide, Volumes 1-3" by Luis D. Aponte.

Criminal activity is the second leading cause of school gun violence, not lack of prayer. One often overlooked statistic is the prevalence of crime on school grounds. Criminal activities, including gang-related conflicts, robbery attempts, and drug deals gone wrong, account for 15.2% of reported school shootings. There is no evidence to support claims that a lack of prayer in schools contributes to shootings. In fact, Christian schools are not immune to gun violence; between 1990 and 2019, there were at least 24 shootings at such institutions. One of the most recent mass school shootings occurred at Covenant School, a private Christian elementary school in Nashville, Tennessee, on March 23, 2023. According to reports, a 28-year-old former student was responsible for the tragic event. Seven people were killed: three children, three adults, and the shooter, who was shot by police, making it the worst school shooting in Tennessee's history.[4] One of the victims of the Covenant School shooting was the 9-year-old daughter of a pastor at Covenant Presbyterian Church.[5]

Another mass shooting at Abundant Life Christian School in Madison, Wisconsin on December 16, 2024, was equally tragic. A 15-year-old former female student killed a teacher and a student, injured six others, and then took her own life at this private Christian school, which serves about 420 students.[6][7] In each of these tragic cases, the shooters were former students at schools that supported the practice of prayer.

Moreover, at least 47 shooters, including the Parkland perpetrator, had a Christian background.[8] These findings highlight the need for consistent police presence in schools to deter criminal behavior. Communities and parents can counter criminal activity and gang influence through Community Violence Intervention (CVI) programs and by providing after-school programs that channel children's energy, foster self-worth, and promote emotional resilience. Faith organizations should view this as a call to action to collaborate with communities to help reduce youth gun violence.

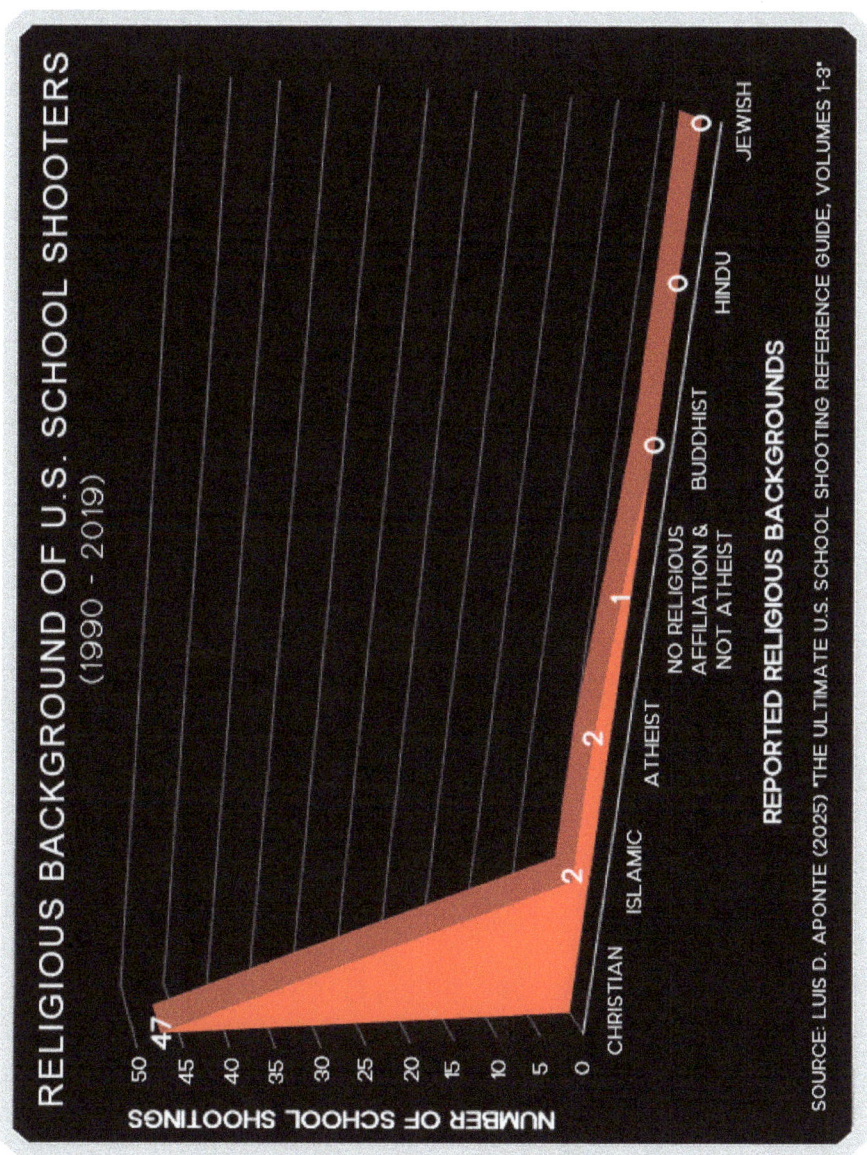

Religious backgrounds of U.S. school shooters (1990-2019).
Infographic created by Harrison Snell and Luis D. Aponte. Based on "The Ultimate U.S. School Shooting Reference Guide, Volumes 1-3" by Luis D. Aponte.

Accidental shootings and self-defense rank third in school gun violence incidents, not video games. While guns are glamorized in entertainment media, other developed nations with similar access to video games, music, movies, TV and streaming shows experience far lower gun violence rates than the U.S. For many teens, guns represent an exciting yet dangerous novelty, leading them to bring unsecured firearms to school. Firearms can also be seen as an equalizer for students who feel threatened or bullied. As a result, 13.7% of U.S. school shootings are accidental or involve self-defense. Accidental discharges occur when students show off a gun to friends, store it in a backpack for protection, or when school personnel mishandle their firearms. One tragic example of an accidental firearm discharge occurred at Ross Elementary School on April 19, 2011. A 6-year-old boy found a .380-caliber semi-automatic gun under a futon cushion at home and brought it to school. The gun fell out of the student's pocket and discharged, injuring himself and two other children aged five and six.[9] [10] These incidents highlight the need for educating both children and adults on safe firearm storage and handling in order to prevent accidents. Offering self-defense classes, along with encouraging open communication with school counselors, could help teen and young adult students build confidence and self-discipline, thus reducing the perceived need for firearms.

Many motivations for school gun violence remain unknown or underreported. The motivations behind approximately 30.9% of school shootings remain unclear, presenting a significant challenge for schools and law enforcement. On April 16, 2007, 23-year-old Seung-Hui Cho brought a .22-caliber Walther P22 handgun, a 9mm Glock 19 handgun, and nearly 400 rounds of ammunition to Virginia Tech in Blacksburg, Virginia.[11] During this horrific event, Cho killed 32 students and instructors and injured 17 others before taking his own life. Reports speculated on various motivations, including violent video games and psychiatric medication.[12] Additionally, over 465 U.S. suspects remain at large from school shooting incidents that occurred between 1990 and 2019, making it exceedingly challenging to decipher their motives. Identifying these motivations is essential for fostering safer and more supportive environments for students. To prevent future shootings, collaboration among students, parents, schools, Community Violence Intervention (CVI) programs, and youth-focused nonprofits may hold the key.

9

Overlooked Warning Signs

Marjory Stoneman Douglas High School, named after the environmental activist who fought to preserve the Florida Everglades, still holds her spirit of activism. Seven years after the 2018 mass shooting, the school's alumni and parents continue the fight to ensure its safety. To break the cycle of gun violence, the question remains: "How do we prevent the next school shooting?" History shows that many shooters exhibited warning signs long before escalating to gun violence, yet these signs were often overlooked or underreported. Every community member must recognize and act on these warning indications to prevent tragedies, without infringing on constitutional rights. My research into 1,204 U.S. school shootings from 1990 to 2019 identifies the most common warning signs.

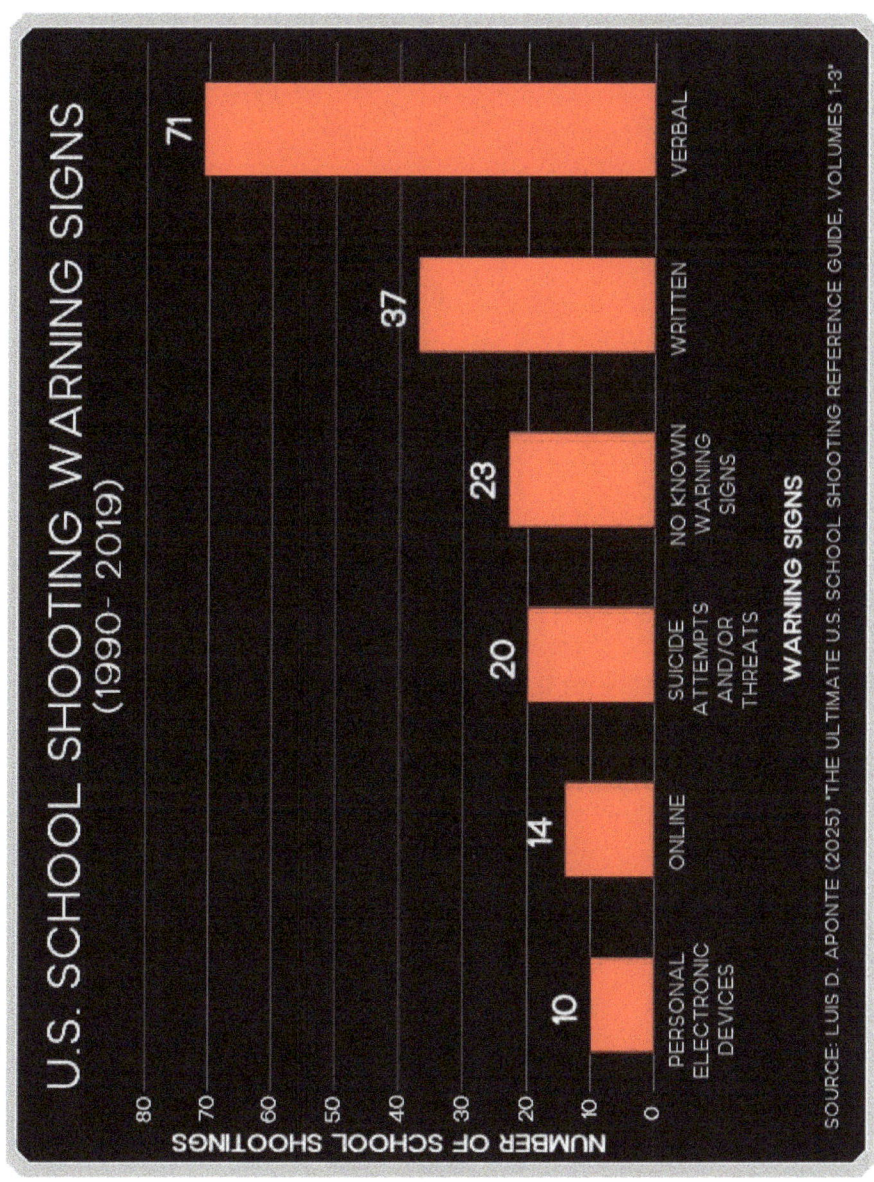

U.S. school shooting warning signs (1990-2019).
Infographic created by Luis D. Aponte. Based on "The Ultimate U.S. School Shooting Reference Guide, Volumes 1-3" by Luis D. Aponte.

Verbal warning signs are often the last chance to intervene before tragedy strikes. In at least 71 school shootings, someone knew about the attack beforehand. For example, in the 1998 Westside Middle School shooting, reports indicated two shooters, Mitchell Scott Johnson, aged 11, and Andrew Douglas Golden, aged 13, killed five people and injured 10 more. They openly discussed their plans, with one chillingly declaring, "Tomorrow you will find out if you live or die," and "I have a lot of killing to do."[1] Another student allegedly overheard the second shooter plotting to bring guns to school and informed his father, who notified the school counselor. Tragically, it was too late to stop the attack.

Written warning signs often reveal a shooter's escalating thoughts and plans. Investigations into at least 37 incidents have shown that shooters documented their intentions in hit lists, journals, poems, essays, wills, or suicide letters. In 2006, the Jefferson County sheriff in Colorado released nearly 1,000 pages of documents seized from the homes of the Columbine High School killers–specifically, journals kept by shooters Eric Harris and Dylan Klebold–following a lawsuit filed by The Denver Post. Harris' journal entries express his admiration for Nazis and swastikas, his admission of being a racist, his hatred of his own appearance, his lack of self-esteem, and his desire to kill and instill fear in others.[2,3]

One glaring red flag in Harris' journal, dated October 23, 1998, was the following statement: "Once I finally start my killing, keep this in mind, there are probably about 100 people max in the school alone who I don't want to die, the rest, MUST F*****G DIE! If I didn't like you or if you pissed me off and lived through my attacks, consider yourself one lucky g*d d**n N****R."[4,5]

Once I finally start my killing spree this in mind, there are probably about 100 people max in the school alone who I don't want to die, the rest, MUST P------ G DIE! elf it didn't like you or if you pissed me off and lived through my attacks; consider yourselfs one lucky god d----- N-----. Pity that a lot of the dead will lives wastes in someways, like dead lil chicken who were still v-----, they could have been good f--. oh well, too f------ bad. life don't fair.... not by a long f---- shot when I'm at the wheel, too. God I want to torch and level everything in this whole f------ area but bombs of that size are hard to make, and plus I would need a f------ fully loaded A10 to get every store on Wadsworth and all the buildings downtown. heh, Imagine THAT ya f-----, picture half of denver on fire just from me and Vodka. ------ napalm on sides of skyscrapers and car garages blowing up from exploded gas tanks....oh man that would be beautiful. ~10/23/98

"Columbine Documents" released by the Jefferson County Sheriff's Office.
Image courtesy of The Internet Archive, 2017, p. JC-001-026013.

In the Virginia Tech mass shooting on April 16, 2007, 23-year-old student, Seung-Hui Cho killed 32 and injured 17 before killing himself. After the Columbine mass shooting in 1999, Cho's middle school teachers noted his writing expressed thoughts of suicide and homicide, indicating that "he wanted to repeat Columbine."[6] In 2006, Cho even wrote a detailed fictional account of a school shooting involving a character who wanted to kill everyone in his school.[7] Taking these written signs seriously can save lives by enabling communities to address concerns before they escalate into violence.

Social media and online forums often become platforms for shooters to share their thoughts as a last resort. At least 14 school shooters posted their plans online, while 10 used personal electronic devices to text, call, or document their intentions. The 2018 Marjory Stoneman Douglas High School shooter, Nikolas Jacob Cruz, who killed 17 and injured 17, posted on YouTube, "I'm going to be a professional school shooter,"[8] but the FBI couldn't identify him in time. He also posted on Instagram, "I want to kill people."[9] These digital distress signals can be cries for help, and taking them seriously can prevent future tragedies.

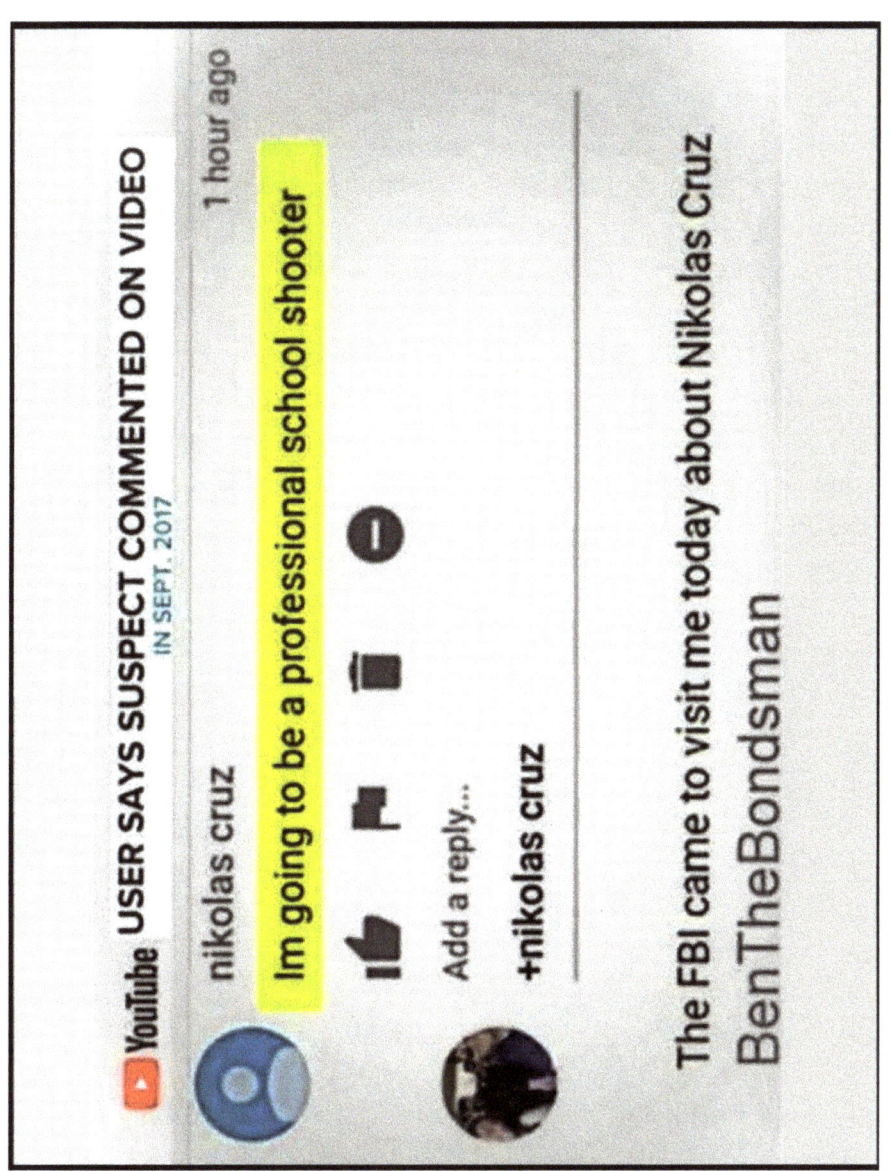

YouTube post by a user named "nikolas cruz" prior to the Parkland mass shooting.
Image courtesy of CBS News, February 15, 2018.

Everyone plays a crucial role in recognizing and addressing warning signs. Being proactive and paying close attention to children's behavior and communication is essential. Creating a safe environment, where children feel comfortable expressing their thoughts, is key. Parents can also use digital tools to monitor their child's online activity. Signs of anxiety, depression, or suicidal thoughts must be taken seriously and may require professional help. One of the most important steps a parent can take is to keep firearms securely locked away from minors.

Nonprofits like Sandy Hook Promise, Make Our Schools Safe, and Stand for the Silent offer additional life-saving resources. Just as Marjory Stoneman Douglas worked tirelessly to preserve the Everglades, communities can prevent future tragedies by staying vigilant and engaged across generations.

10

Most Vulnerable Locations

The aftermath of the 2018 mass shooting at my alma mater in Parkland, Florida, revealed vulnerabilities on campus that I hope will never be exploited again. Watching children go off to school each morning should fill parents with a sense of hope, knowing they are entering a safe environment where learning thrives and friendships form. This confidence relies on trust and transparency. Parents must be aware of potential dangers on school grounds, especially in order to prevent school gun violence. When informed, communities can work together with schools to address risks, ensuring the campus remains a sanctuary. Based on an evaluation of 1,204 U.S. school shootings, the following statistics reveal where incidents most frequently occur.

Back when I was in high school, the parking lot was a social hub where friends showed off cars, shared gossip, and discussed weekend plans. It is distressing to learn that 699 (58%) of all reported school shootings from 1990 to 2019 occurred outdoors on school grounds, with parking lots being a common site, while 399 (33%) took place indoors. Additionally, 115 (9%) of these shooting locations were underreported. Many are unaware of these statistics because incidents involving three or fewer victims rarely receive national attention. Moreover, the Centers for Disease Control and Prevention (CDC) faces restrictions on studying gun violence due to the "Dickey Amendment." This legislation limits the flow of fact-based research on how to prevent future acts of gun violence against children. The prevalence of shootings in outdoor areas highlights the urgent need for improved surveillance and security measures in these vulnerable spots across K-12 and post-secondary schools. Furthermore, it may be in parents' best interest to organize with advocacy groups, contact representatives, collect signatures for petitions, and support political candidates that support overturning the "Dickey Amendment," while supporting other school safety initiatives, such as "Alyssa's Law."

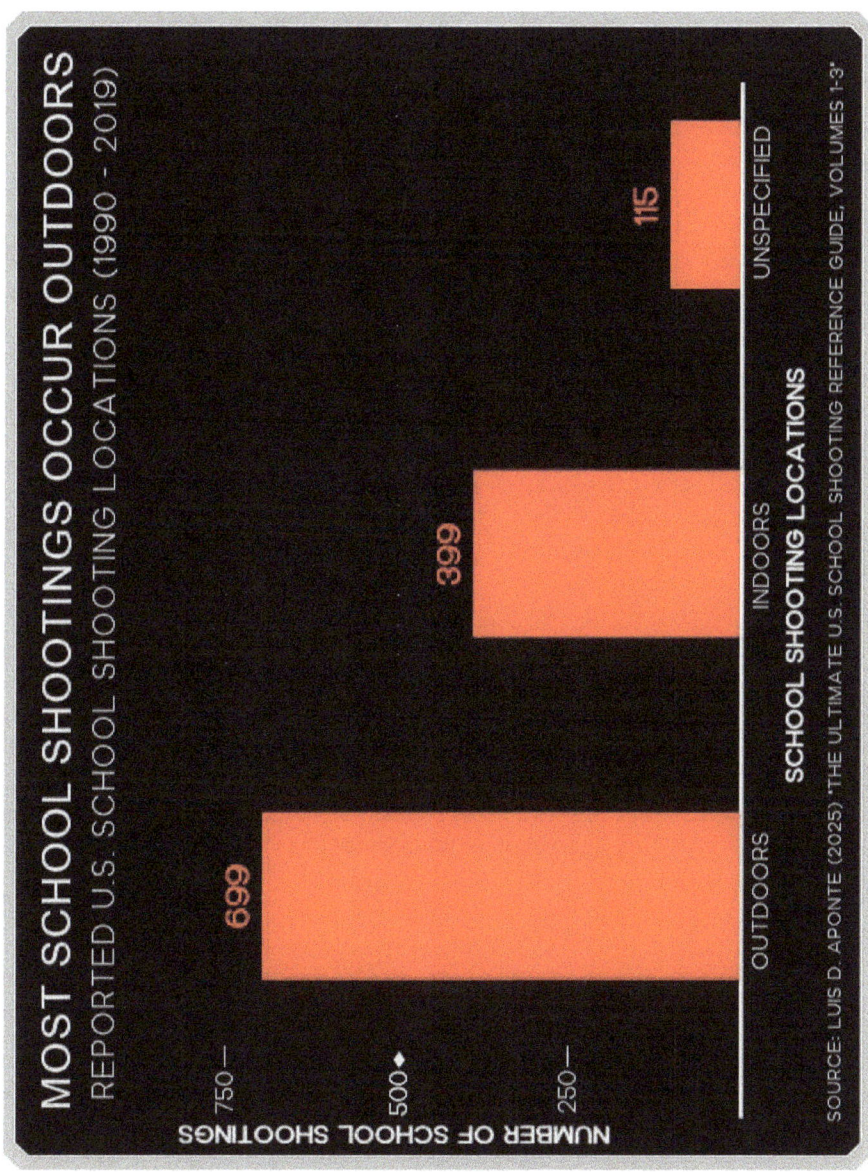

Most school shootings occur outdoors. Reported U.S. school shooting locations (1990-2019).

Infographic created by Harrison Snell and Luis D. Aponte. Based on "The Ultimate U.S. School Shooting Reference Guide, Volumes 1-3" by Luis D. Aponte.

K-12 schools form the foundation of children's education, shaping their beliefs about the world and their potential role in it. While academics, friendships, and future goals often take center stage, it's easy to overlook daily security risks. Football stadiums and parking lots, basketball courts, and bus stops are the most common outdoor locations for shootings in K-12 schools, accounting for 59.5% of outdoor incidents. Conversely, some of the safest places during an outdoor shooting are volleyball courts (0.7%), handball courts (1.4%), and tennis courts (1.4%).

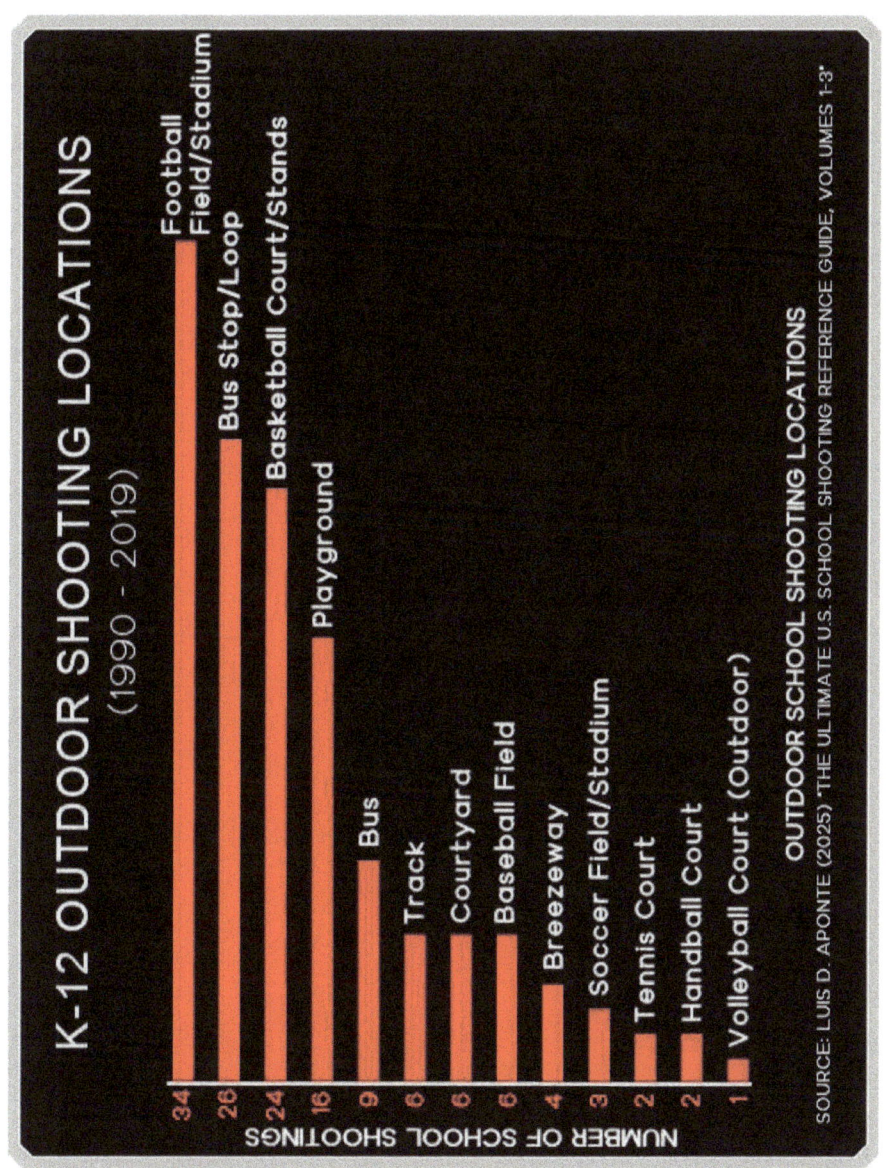

Outdoor U.S. school shooting locations (K-12) (1990-2019).
Infographic created by Harrison Snell and Luis D. Aponte. Based on "The Ultimate U.S. School Shooting Reference Guide, Volumes 1-3" by Luis D. Aponte.

Classrooms, hallways, and bathrooms are the most common indoor locations for shootings in K-12 schools, accounting for 63.2% of indoor incidents. Alternatively, some of the safest places during an indoor shooting are maintenance areas (0.4%), computer labs (0.4%), and libraries (0.8%). These historical statistics may be helpful to parents, students, educators and law enforcement in the event of an active school shooting crisis.

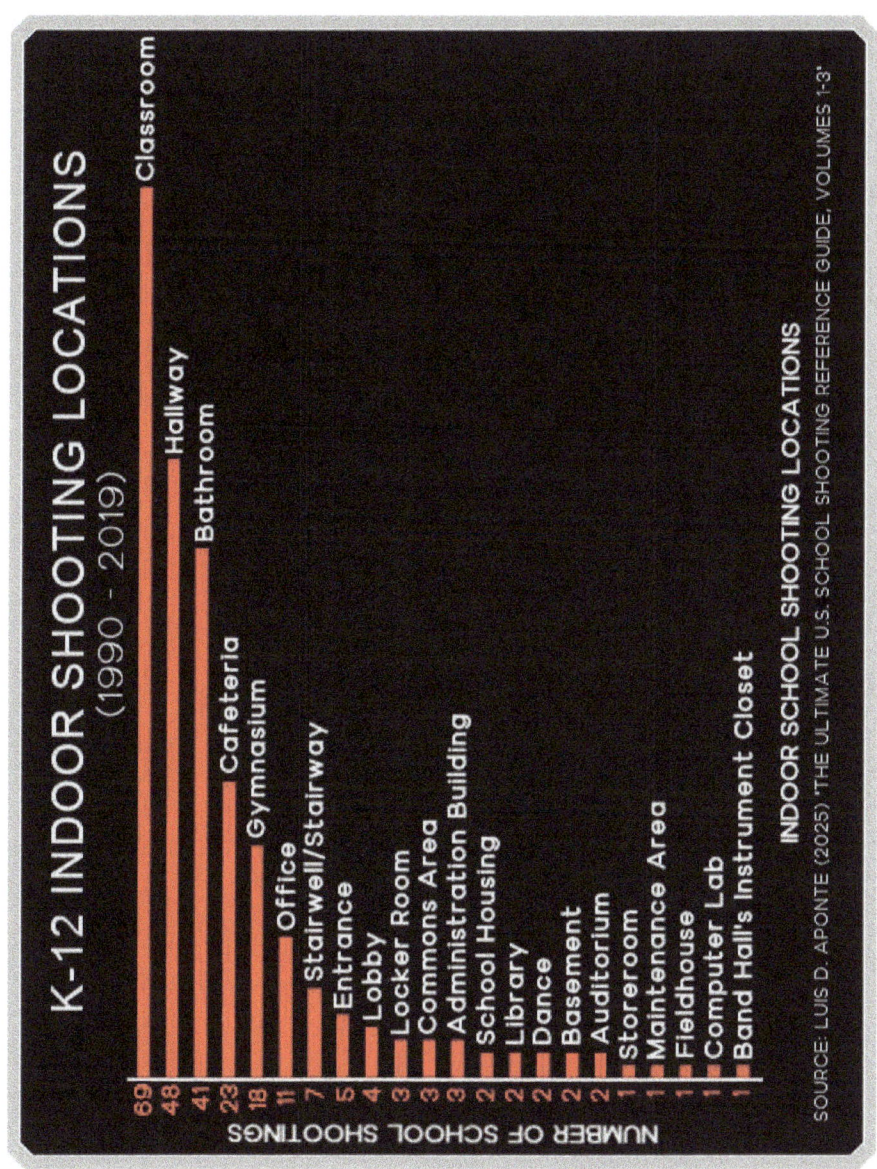

Indoor U.S. school shooting locations (K-12) (1990-2019).
Infographic created by Harrison Snell and Luis D. Aponte. Based on "The Ultimate U.S. School Shooting Reference Guide, Volumes 1-3" by Luis D. Aponte.

Colleges and universities are places where young adults pursue dreams, develop critical thinking, and build professional networks. Despite their revered status, postsecondary institutions have their own risks. For example, 50.58% of all reported shootings at postsecondary schools from 1990-2019 occurred outdoors. Of the known outdoor shootings, 100 (57.8%) of all outdoor shootings were at unspecified locations. Notably, 71 (41%) were at a parking lot or garage. In contrast, only 1 shooting (0.5%) took place at a cookout, and 1 (0.5%) occurred at a bus stop/bench. It is significant to note that the many of the shootings that took place at a parking lot took place next to a student housing area.

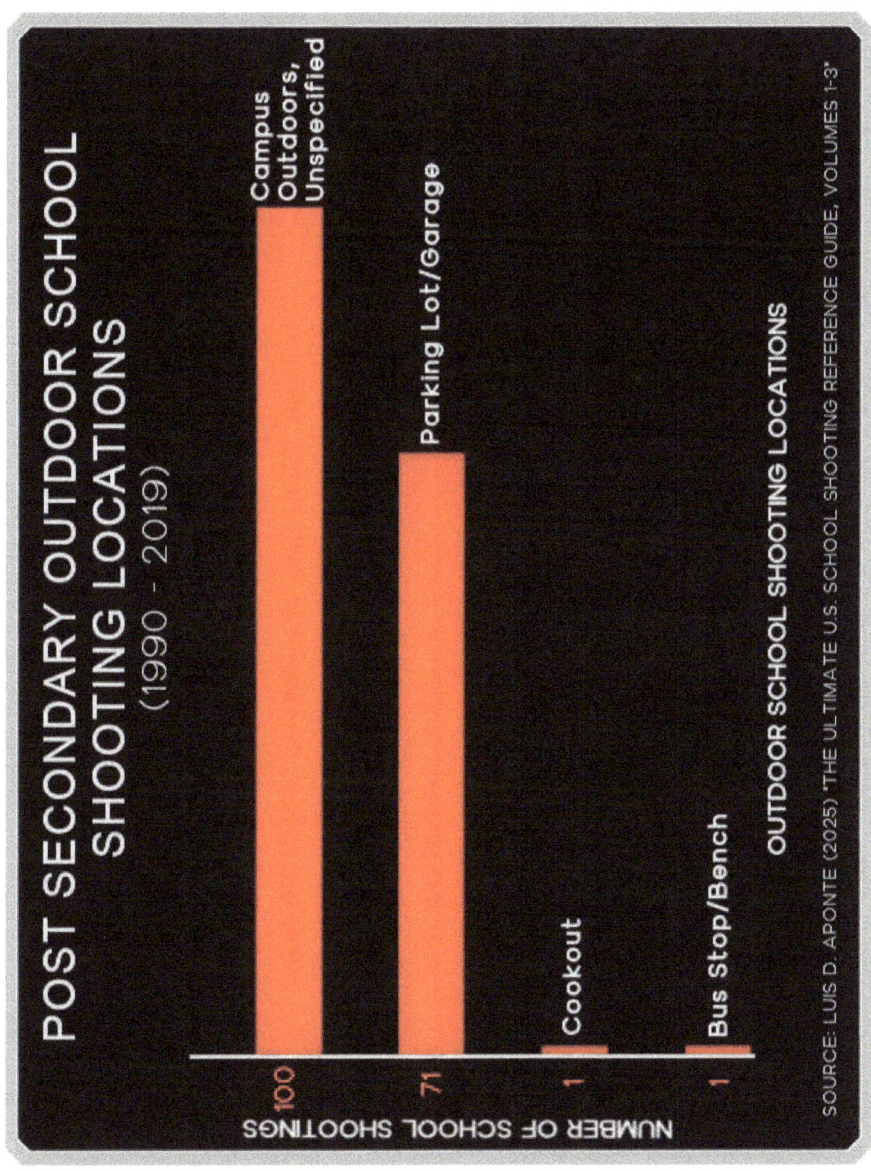

Outdoor U.S. school shooting locations (Post Secondary) (1990-2019).
Infographic created by Luis D. Aponte. Based on "The Ultimate U.S. School Shooting Reference Guide, Volumes 1-3" by Luis D. Aponte.

Student housing, academic buildings, and classrooms are the most vulnerable indoor post-secondary school locations, making up 80.5% of indoor incidents on campuses. Statistically, the safest areas during indoor shootings include student lounges (0.67%), computer rooms (0.67%), and bookstores (0.67%). These findings emphasize the need for comprehensive safety protocols targeting these high-risk zones. Moreover, parents should carefully reevaluate allowing their children to live in student housing due to the apparent lack of security on many university and college campuses, both indoors and outdoors. Prioritizing your child's safety involves taking a closer look at the measures–or lack thereof–being implemented to protect them.

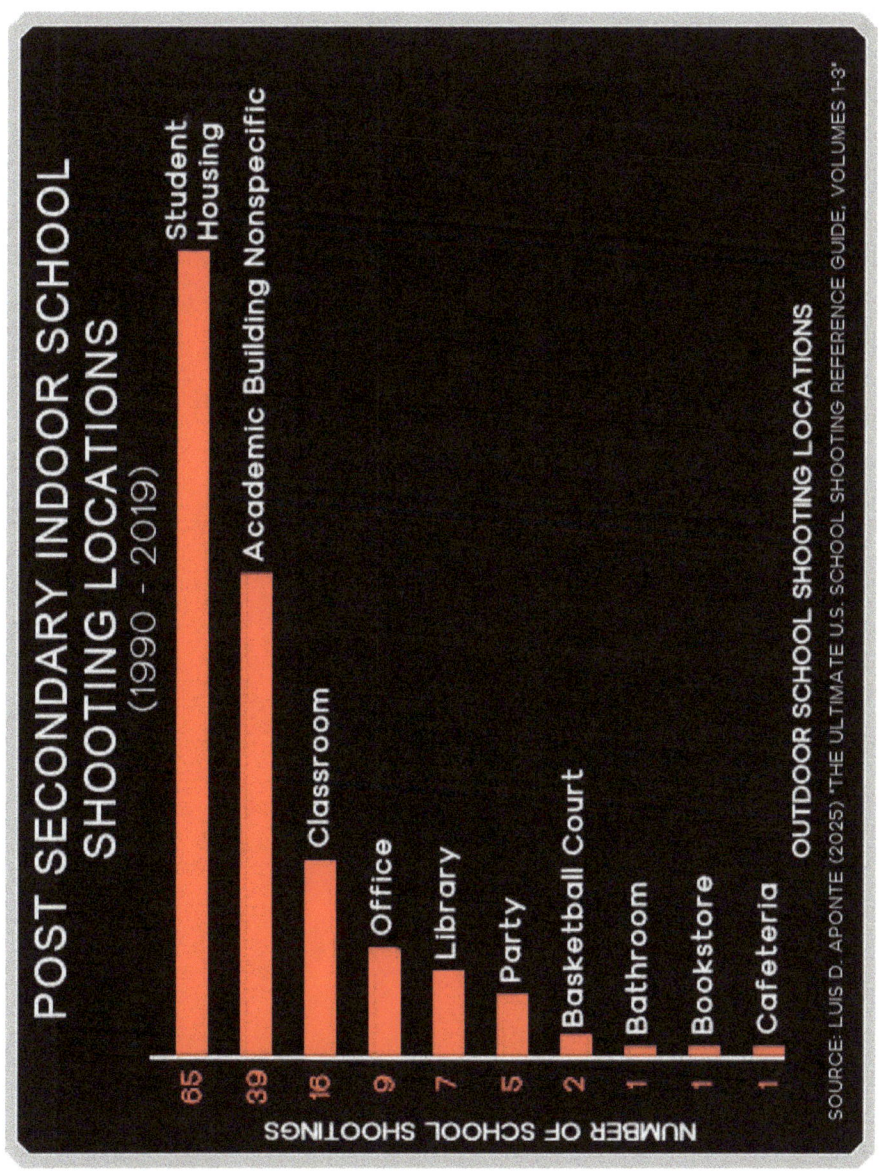

Indoor U.S. school shooting locations (Post Secondary) (1990-2019).
Infographic created by Luis D. Aponte. Based on "The Ultimate U.S. School Shooting Reference Guide, Volumes 1-3" by Luis D. Aponte.

Staying informed about school safety is crucial for parents. Parents can attend PTA meetings, familiarize themselves with emergency procedures, and encourage children to take safety drills seriously. It's also essential to teach young people to be cautious about sharing their location online. Maintaining open conversations about their experiences and any safety concerns is key. Reputable smartphone apps that provide school safety updates and enable kids to report local incidents can be valuable tools. By being proactive, engaged, and a little tech-savvy, parents can help create a safer environment for their children.

11

Mass vs. Conventional School Shootings

The common misperception and underrepresentation of school shooting patterns may stem from national reporting that focuses primarily on mass school shooting events with numerous victims, rather than on conventional school shootings with three or fewer victims. Smaller shooting events are rarely reported in national news, contributing to the dangerous illusion that gun violence in schools is a minor problem. Admittedly, school shootings are statistically rare events, considering there are over 100,000 K-12 and post-secondary schools in the United States. While these incidents may not have the same national security implications as foreign terrorist attacks, dedicating resources to understanding and addressing the root causes of school gun violence can help increase public confidence in the safety of schools and in our elected officials.

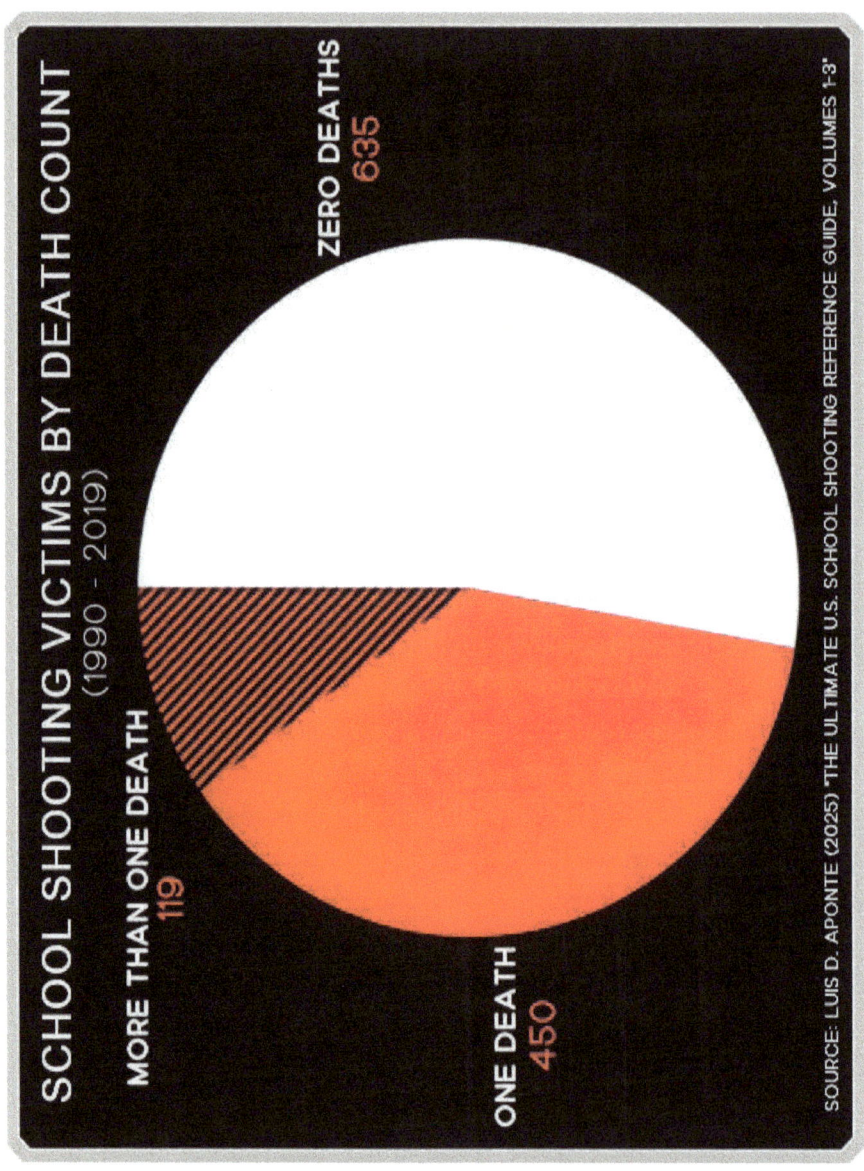

U.S. school shooting victims by death count (1990-2019).
Infographic created by Luis D. Aponte. Based on "The Ultimate U.S. School Shooting

Moreover, confusing and inconsistent definitions of mass shootings exacerbate this issue. According to the federal Investigative Assistance for Violent Crimes Act of 2012, mass killings are defined as three or more killings in a single incident.[1] Alternatively, the FBI defines a mass shooting as any incident where at least four people are killed with a gun.[2] Several sources argue that this definition does not include the shooter. Gun violence researcher Dr. Garen Wintemute of the University of California at Davis suggests there is no legal definition of a mass shooting.[3] Consequently, the FBI's definition excludes several mass shooting events where four or more people were shot but not killed, diminishing the seriousness of these incidents and invalidating the shooter as a human statistic. This oversight ignores the trauma, harm, and injustice inflicted on survivors of gun violence, minimizing the public's understanding of the grave threat posed by gun violence in the United States.

To provide communities and researchers with a comprehensive understanding of gun violence in schools, I propose a more inclusive definition of a mass shooting: an incident in which at least four individuals are shot with a firearm, either injured or killed, including any alleged shooter(s) who may also have been shot during or immediately after the incident. This definition, distinct from that of a mass killing, which focuses only on the number of fatalities, includes all individuals affected by the shooting. By acknowledging the true scope of these tragedies, we can better address the pervasive issue of gun violence in the United States.

Using this definition, statistics from 85 mass school shootings reveal a similar pattern to conventional shootings, with a few stark differences. The most common age range among mass school shooters is 14 to 20, while the most frequently targeted ages in these shootings are 6, and 14 to 20. (Note: This is based on the best available information from reporting. The ages of 245 victims were not reported.) Conversely, the most common age range among all school shooting suspects is 13 to 25, with the most targeted age groups being 6, and

13 to 26. Between 2013 and 2015, a study conducted by Everytown for Gun Safety Support Fund still found that over half of the shooters obtained the gun used in the attack from their home, "likely because an adult did not store it locked and unloaded."[4] These findings underscore a critical and immediate need: preventing underage access to firearms is essential to preventing a significant bulk of future school shootings, though it will not prevent all cases.

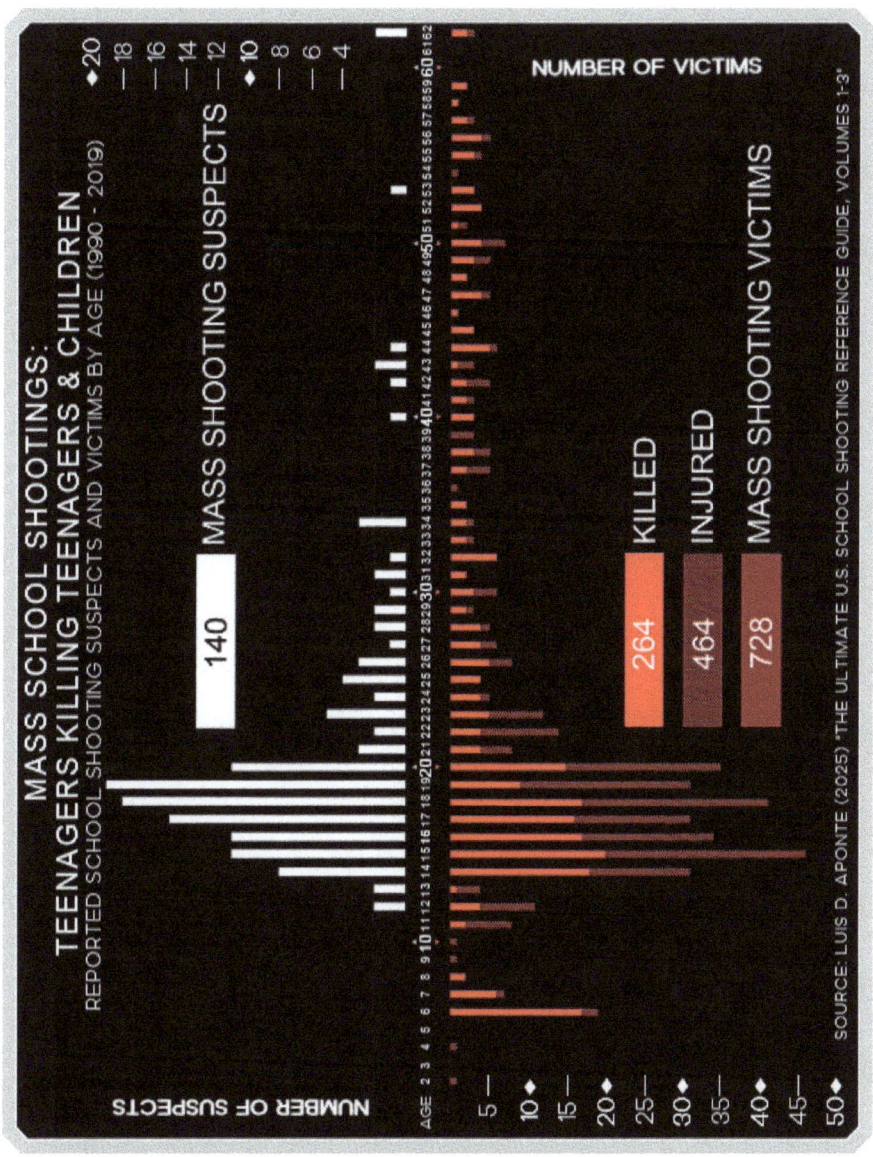

Mass U.S. school shootings: teenagers killing teenagers and children (1990-2019).
Infographic created by Harrison Snell and Luis D. Aponte. Based on "The Ultimate U.S. School Shooting Reference Guide, Volumes 1-3" by Luis D. Aponte.

Thirty mass school shootings had motivations that were either unknown, unreported, or featured conflicting information. However, among the reported motivations, the most common factors were fights, feuds, arguments, and disputes. These were followed by rejection, protesting authority, and bullying. This data suggests that teaching emotional mastery skills and conflict resolution skills to children, as well as introducing Community Violence Intervention (CVI) programs in local neighborhoods, are the minimum strategies needed to prevent the largest number of school gun violence incidents. "CVI strategies are a key component of the public safety ecosystem, working to prevent violence rather than punish people after the fact," said David Muhammad, Executive Director of the National Institute for Criminal Justice Reform.[5] Prioritizing these preventative measures can ensure our schools become sanctuaries of safety and growth for all students.

Additionally, resource officers, teachers, and coaches are role models on campus, especially for troubled youth. These leaders are on the front lines of this ongoing battle and are the most underrated and unsung heroes who deserve our support. Students are the greatest source of intelligence when it comes to preventing violence in schools. As a result, stronger bonds of trust are needed between adults and students so that children feel comfortable and safe enough to speak up and help save lives, anonymously. Supporting and investing in the development of these professionals on the frontlines is crucial to fostering a secure and caring school environment.

Whether you, a loved one, or an acquaintance struggles with emotional or mental health issues, have the courage to seek professional help. Recognizing when you or someone you love needs support takes courage, and accepting that help yourself takes even greater strength. If you're facing challenges like depression, bullying, rejection, relationship issues, divorce, school or work difficulties, or financial problems, professional counseling or therapy can be a lifesaver. You may not feel that anyone cares during your darkest hour, but there are people who love you and truly want to help. You can and will get through this difficult time and become stronger. Be patient and give the process as much time as you need. Surround yourself with positive and supportive people. Let go of anyone who drains light from your life. By fostering a culture of mutual respect and open communication, we can transform our schools into beacons of safety and compassion.

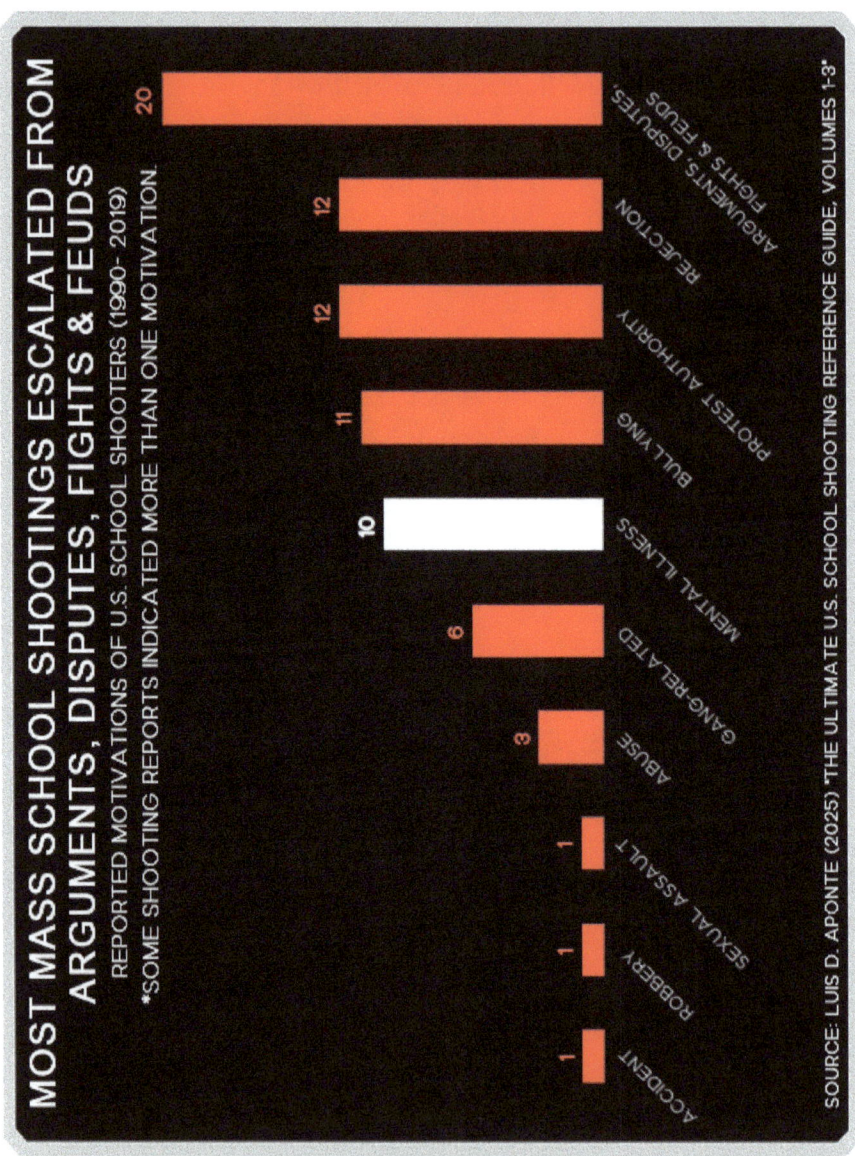

Most mass school shootings escalated from fights, feuds, arguments and disputes. Reported motivations of U.S. school shooters (1990-2019).

Infographic created by Luis D. Aponte. Based on "The Ultimate U.S. School Shooting Reference Guide, Volumes 1-3" by Luis D. Aponte.

Handguns are the most frequently used firearms in mass school shootings, accounting for 67.4% of identified weapons. Their compact size allows minors to easily steal them from home and conceal them in backpacks or clothing. Tragic events at schools, such as Virginia Tech, Santana High School, and West Nickel Mines Amish School, illustrate the devastating impact of this accessibility. Due to inconsistent metal detector use and inadequate monitoring of alternate access points in schools, potential shooters carrying small firearms often go unnoticed. A balanced approach begins with securing firearms at home to prevent access by minors and theft. Additionally, consistent metal detector use, monitoring alternative school access points with community volunteer assistance, comprehensive mental health support, anti-bullying initiatives, and community engagement programs can collectively nurture and raise a safer school environment.

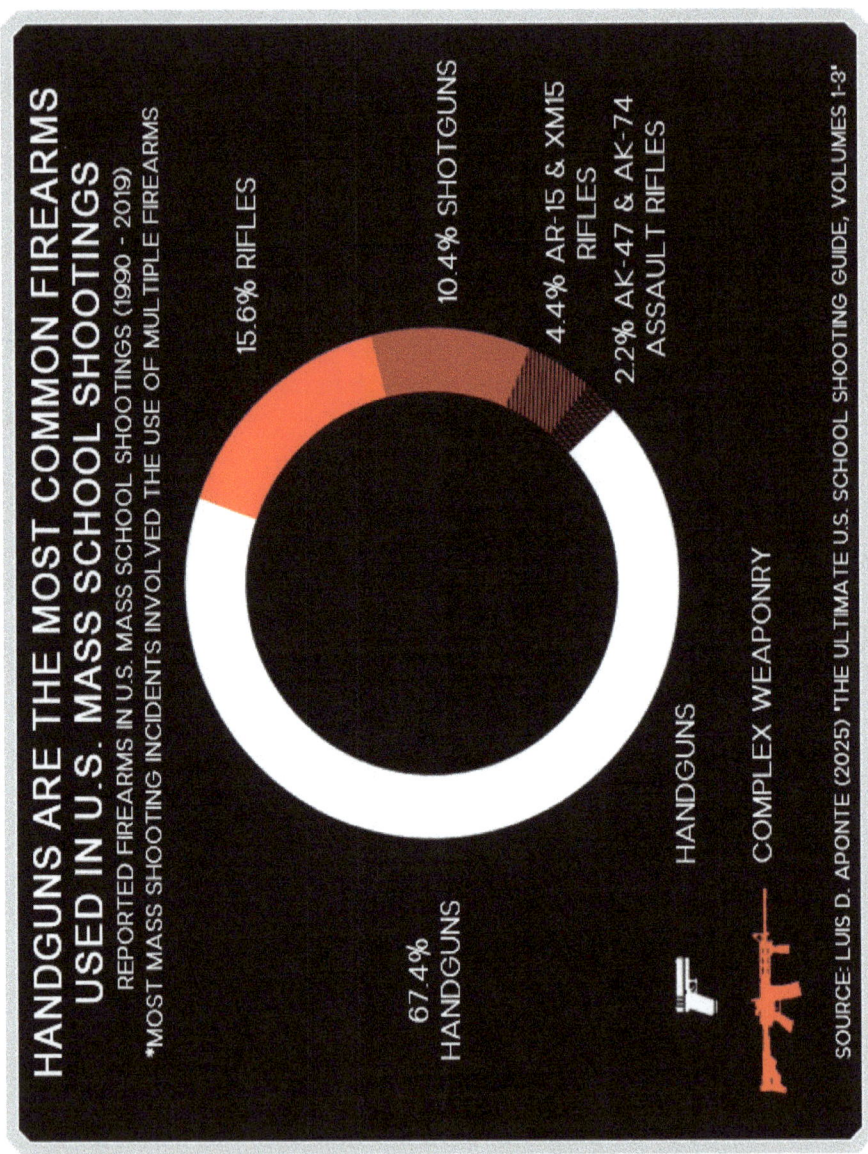

Handguns are the most common firearms used in U.S. mass school shootings. Reported firearms in U.S. mass school shootings (1990-2019).

Infographic created by Luis D. Aponte. Based on "The Ultimate U.S. School Shooting Reference Guide, Volumes 1-3" by Luis D. Aponte.

Among the warning signs reported in U.S. mass school shootings, verbal warnings were the most prominent. Multiple incidents revealed that several warning signs, including written and online indications, were present before the tragedies. This highlights the urgent need for parents to monitor their children's journals, electronic devices, class assignments, and online activity. While concerns about privacy invasion, trust issues, and anxiety due to constant surveillance are valid, fostering a family culture of open communication is crucial. Regularly discussing your child's experiences, feelings, and concerns about school, relationships, health, and other life issues can be highly beneficial. With the help of a trained family therapist, families can improve communication and create stronger family bonds. "Adolescents are not monsters. They are just people trying to learn how to make it among the adults in the world, who are probably not so sure themselves," said Virginia Satir, author and psychotherapist often referred to as the "mother of family therapy."[6] Parents and children should jointly establish boundaries and understand the reasons behind certain safety measures. Each family and culture will have unique approaches that work best for them. Balancing safety and privacy can create a supportive and secure environment for children.

Students must take warning signs seriously, whether they come from friends, family, or classmates. Silence can mean the difference between life and death. While concerns about misinterpreting behaviors or creating distrust are valid, the regret of staying silent when a tragedy could have been prevented can be far more haunting. Teaching children to recognize warning signs empowers them to distinguish genuine threats from typical behavior. Encourage them to approach peers with empathy, emphasizing that everyone has bad days, and foster a culture of support rather than judgment. Positive, constructive reporting should focus on helping, not punishing. Remind children that if they feel uncertain, they can always seek guidance from a trusted adult. Ultimately, building awareness, promoting vigilance, avoiding biases, and taking proactive steps are crucial to preventing school shootings. Given limited resources, schools cannot shoulder this responsibility alone. Parents and community leaders must take the lead in these preventative efforts.

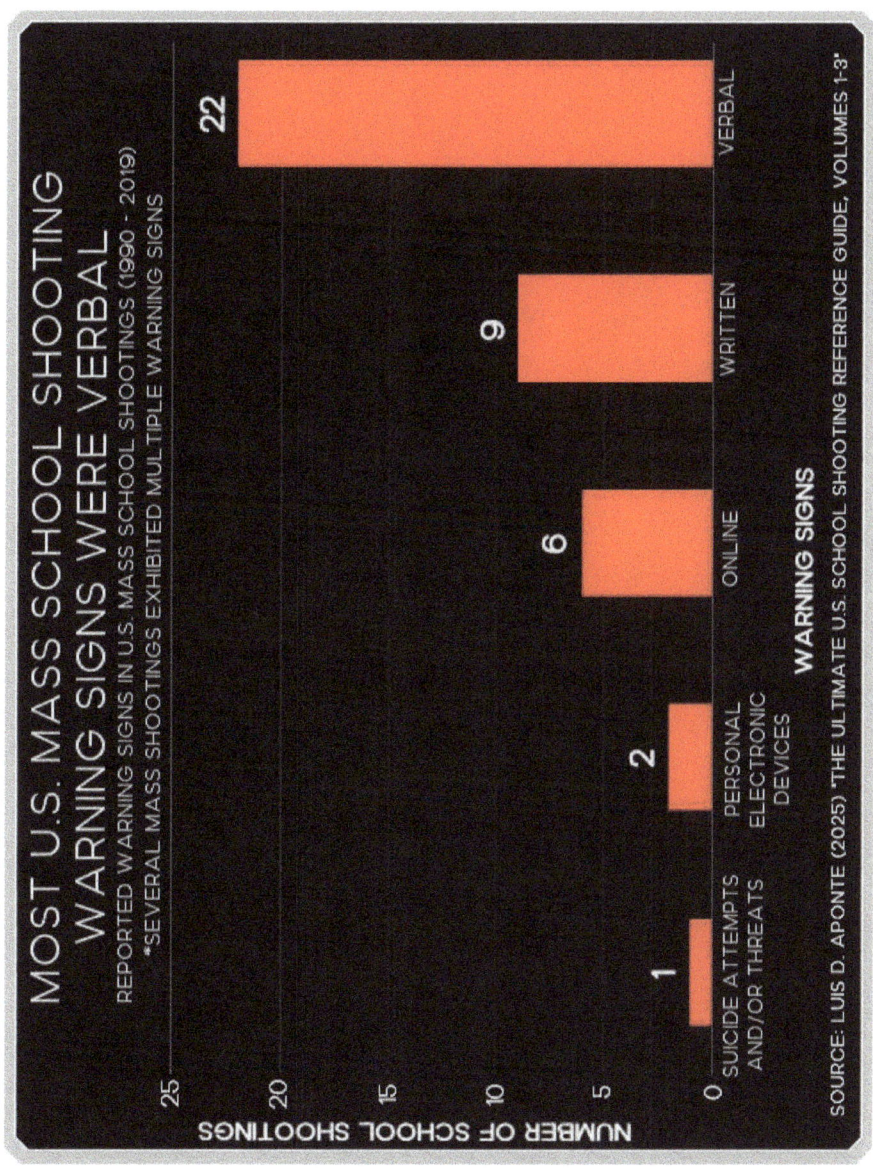

Most mass school shootings warning signs were verbal. Reported warning signs in U.S. mass school shootings (1990-2019).

Infographic created by Luis D. Aponte. Based on "The Ultimate U.S. School Shooting Reference Guide, Volumes 1-3" by Luis D. Aponte.

12

How to Prevent the Next School Shooting

Reports from 1,204 school shootings indicate that arguments, fights, and feuds are the leading causes of school gun violence, accounting for approximately 36.7% of incidents from 1990 to 2019. Contrary to popular belief, statistics indicate that mental illness and bullying are not the primary drivers. This data highlights a crucial yet often overlooked aspect of prevention: the role of emotional intelligence and emotional mastery.

Teaching children and young adults the critical life skill of emotional intelligence can be one of the most important and underestimated tools for preventing gun violence in schools–and violence in general. Emotional intelligence is the ability to understand and manage your own emotions while recognizing and influencing the emotions of those around you.[1] Emotional mastery takes this a step further by ensuring emotions do not dictate actions, allowing for quick recovery from setbacks and maintaining a positive outlook despite challenges.

However, fostering emotional intelligence is perhaps one of the most difficult skills to achieve because it requires being tested in the real world, not merely checking off boxes on paper. Emotional insights empower individuals to drive motivation, develop creative solutions, and engage in proactive behaviors that align with their values and goals. By equipping children with these tools, we enable them to anticipate future needs, changes, and potential problems, rather than merely reacting to events as they occur. This emotional resilience mirrors the Japanese proverb, "Nana-Korobi, Ya-Oki," which translates to "Fall seven times, get up eight," signifying perseverance despite adversity.[2]

The human experience is an emotional rollercoaster for everyone, characterized by the excitement of life's peaks, moments of wonder, the insecurity of not having control, rapid changes, surprising twists, terrifying drops, and the satisfaction of overcoming challenges. Each generation faces relationship issues, conflicts with authority, rivalries, feuds, personal loss, and desires for revenge over perceived insults. Unfortunately, the response to these emotional challenges in schools has increasingly involved the use of firearms in the United States, as documented in this book and *The Ultimate U.S. School Shooting Reference Guide, Volumes 1-3*.

Just like physical fitness requires regular training and dedication, mastering emotions demands consistent effort and intensity. Emotional intelligence and mastery do not imply suppressing emotions, but rather finding healthy ways to express them. This commitment transforms children from being overwhelmed by their emotions to being in control of them. Learning these skills early in life prepares children for the challenges of relationships and school dynamics, as well as the difficulties they will face later in adulthood.

Growing up in a military and martial arts family, I had the privilege of learning from exceptional martial arts masters who emphasized the importance of controlling one's body and emotions, especially in volatile situations. Bruce Lee, one of my favorite martial artists, encapsulated this philosophy in the movie *Enter the Dragon*. When asked, "What is your style?" Lee responded, "My style? You can call it the art of fighting without fighting." This philosophy—being fluid and adaptable like water—emphasizes avoiding unnecessary confrontation while being ready to defend oneself if necessary. By understanding our own feelings and empathizing with others, we can enhance our relationships, protect our mental well-being, and avoid unnecessary violence.

For martial artists, emotional mastery means defusing and walking away from conflicts rather than escalating them, using power and skill judiciously. It's not about demonstrating bravado and chest pounding. This life skill can be nurtured by strong role models, including family members and community leaders. Emphasizing peace and non-violence, emotional mastery is a virtue taught and encouraged by many major religions of the world and represents an ongoing learning process, as new challenges will always arise. For example:

- **Christianity**: "Blessed are the peacemakers, for they will be called children of God." – The Christian Bible, Matthew 5:9

- **Islam**: "The servants of the Most Merciful are those who walk upon the earth easily, and when the ignorant address them [harshly], they say [words of] peace." – The Qur'an, Surah Al-Furqan 25:63

- **Judaism**: "And a wolf shall live with a lamb, and a leopard shall lie with a kid; and a calf and a lion cub and a fatling [shall lie] together, and a small child shall lead them." – Tanakh, The Hebrew Bible, Isaiah 11:6

- **Buddhism**: "All men tremble at punishment, all men love life; remember that thou art like unto them, and do not kill, nor cause slaughter." – Dhammapada, Chapter 10, Verse 130

- **Hinduism**: "The Blessed Lord said: Fearlessness, purification of one's existence, cultivation of spiritual knowledge, charity, self-control, performance of sacrifice, study of the Vedas, austerity and simplicity; nonviolence, truthfulness, freedom from anger; renunciation, tranquility, aversion to faultfinding, compassion and freedom from covetousness; gentleness, modesty and steady determination; vigor, forgiveness, fortitude, cleanliness, freedom from envy and the passion for honor—these transcendental qualities, O son of Bharata, belong to godly men endowed with divine nature." — Bhagavad Gita 16:1-3

Dr. Martin Luther King Jr.'s iconic "I Have a Dream" speech remains a timeless beacon for racial equality, justice, and peaceful coexistence. His powerful message also intertwined the principles of peace, nonviolence, and emotional mastery, calling for change with dignity and discipline. A striking example of Dr. King's unwavering commitment to nonviolence is encapsulated in his words:

"In the process of gaining our rightful place, we must not be guilty of wrongful deeds. Let us not seek to satisfy our thirst for freedom by drinking from the cup of bitterness and hatred. We must forever conduct our struggle on the high plane of dignity and discipline. We must not allow our creative protest to degenerate into physical violence. Again and again, we must rise to the majestic heights of meeting physical force with soul force."

As a librarian with a deep passion for biographies and history, I am troubled by the idea that political considerations could limit American children's opportunity to explore the rich nuances of our nation's past and learn from great leaders like Dr. King. By encouraging parents, teachers, and community leaders to collaborate in reflecting on past tragedies and fostering emotional resilience from an early age, we can create safer, more harmonious school environments.

The following proposals to reduce school gun violence are based on statistical patterns observed in 1,204 school shootings in the 50 United States and Washington D.C. from 1990 to 2019. However, they do not include data from U.S. territories such as Puerto Rico, U.S. Virgin Islands, American Samoa, Guam, or the Northern Mariana Islands.

1. Introduce emotional intelligence and mastery skills.

Arguments and taunting over sports competitions are as old as the sports are themselves. However, on September 14, 1995, students from Shawnee Mission North and Olathe North High School clashed during a football game between the two schools in Olathe, Kansas. It was a Friday night brimming with rivalry. Tensions escalated quickly—taunting led to a fistfight among students.[3] The animosity didn't stop there. By Sunday night, the feud reignited in the school parking lot, involving around 40 youths.[4] In the chaos, 17-year-old Alfred Jerome Williams Jr. fired a .22-caliber Jennings semiautomatic handgun from a car into the crowd, tragically killing 15-year-old Wilson Montenegro and 19-year-old Jerrell Frazier, and injuring four others.[5][6] After a long court battle, Williams was sentenced to life in prison.

It is crucial for role models—parents and athletic coaches alike—to teach children the importance of sportsmanship and emotional mastery. While friendly banter may add to the spirit of the game, allowing rivalry to escalate into violence risks profound and lasting tragedies.

Between 1990 and 2019, most school shootings were violent reactions to negative emotional experiences. These included disputes, feuds, fights, bullying, depression, rejection, defiance of authority, peer pressure from gang members, and various forms of abuse—sexual, mental, and physical. Equipping children and young adults with essential nonviolent skills, such as anger management and conflict resolution, paired with mental wellness education for K-12 and college students, could empower them to seek alternatives to violence. This approach is also recommended by Dr. James L. Knoll IV and Dr. George D. Annas in the American Psychiatric Association Publishing report *Mass Shootings and Mental Illness*.[7]

Admittedly, this is a difficult request to make of schools that already have limited resources, staff, and time. Schools are hard-pressed to focus on academic priorities and basic safety measures. Moreover, many parents may feel that emotional education should be the responsibility of the family, not the school. Cultural differences may also play a role in defining emotional intelligence. Consequently, it is understandable that allocating time and funds to emotional intelligence programs may be viewed as less essential compared to other pressing needs. After all, we are only trying to save the lives of children and educators.

However, many of these violent outcomes could have potentially been prevented by learning coping and social skills, social-emotional skills, such as empathy and compassion, focusing on positive mental health, and having a network of supportive friends and peers that can help transform negative emotions into constructive and empowering experiences. This is an essential initiative that could be organized periodically as a shared community effort and an opportunity for adults to establish stronger bonds with children and young adults.

If you're looking to explore emotional intelligence further, these books offer valuable insights: *Emotional Intelligence: Why It Can Matter More Than IQ* by Daniel Goleman and *Emotional Intelligence 2.0* by Travis Bradberry and Jean Greaves.

2. Each school should have at least one full-time trained and armed police officer or security guard for every 1,000 students.

Six and a half minutes–that is how quickly 17 lives were lost and 17 others were injured during Florida's deadliest school shooting on February 14, 2018. This tragedy unfolded in a school filled with approximately 3,500 students. According to news reports, the campus had only one armed school resource officer assigned to protect it.[8] Given the critical nature of every second, it is reasonable to assert that having one trained and armed police officer or security guard willing to immediately engage any shooter(s) for every 1,000 students present at school is essential.

Research from the National Center for Education Statistics reveals that only about 46.7% of public schools had sworn law enforcement officers present at least once per week from 2017-2018.[9] School administrators, parents, and law enforcement should collaborate to effectively implement increased SRO presence in schools, while aiming to prevent the exacerbation of the school-to-prison pipeline. The primary goal of this enhanced presence is to enable SROs to save children's lives in critical situations, including active shooter incidents. As a result, officials should consider placing one armed and trained resource officer per 1,000 students at each school in order to enhance safety. Every second matters in a deadly active shooter situation.

Similar to the Parkland massacre in 2018, most school shootings conclude within a few brief minutes. Often, the shooter either commits suicide afterward or has already fled the scene before the police arrive. Out of 1,204 school shootings documented in *The Ultimate U.S. School Shooting Reference Guide, Volumes 1-3*, there were at least:

- 84 suspects apprehended within one week.
- 35 suspects apprehended within one month.
- 45 suspects apprehended within one year.
- 7 suspects apprehended beyond one year.
- 465 suspects who were never apprehended by authorities.
- The rest were either never specified in reporting or the suspects committed suicide.

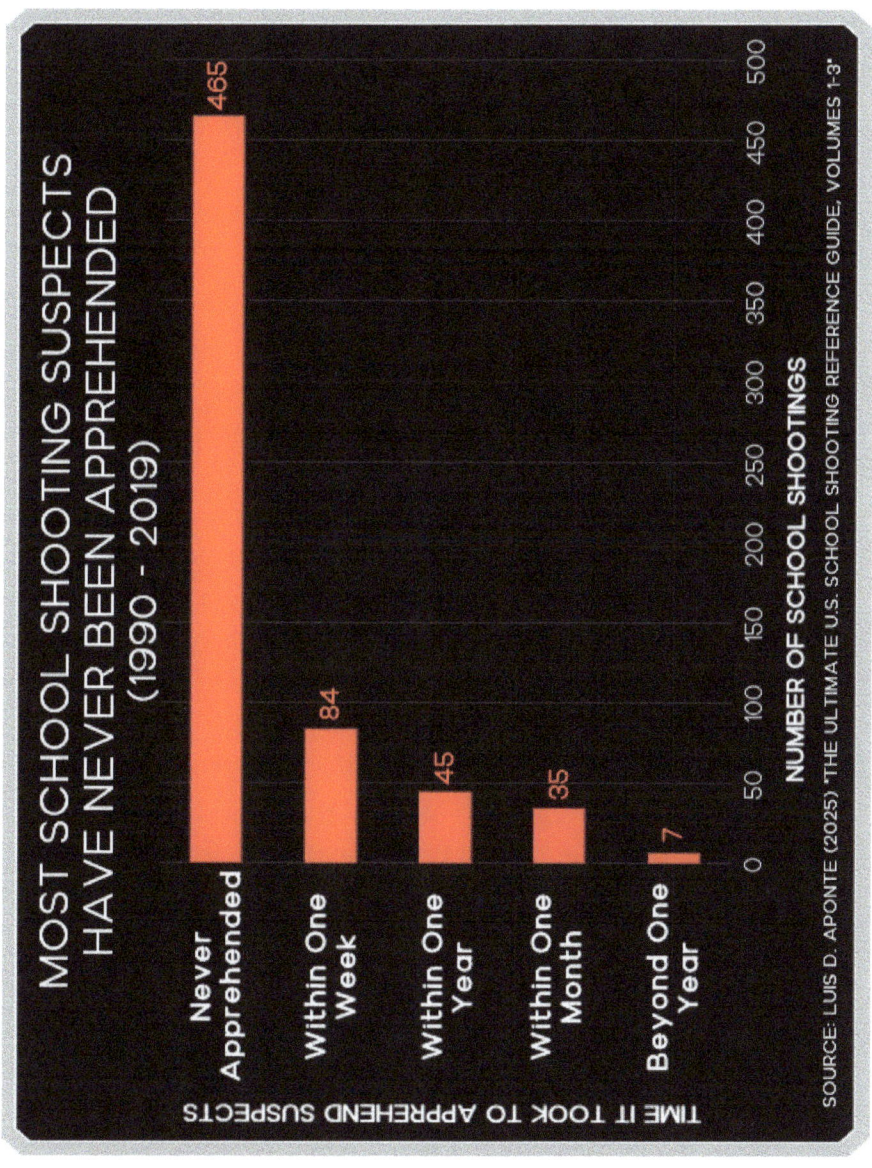

Most school shooting suspects have never been apprehended (1990-2019).
Infographic created by Luis D. Aponte. Based on "The Ultimate U.S. School Shooting Reference Guide, Volumes 1-3" by Luis D. Aponte.

For effective prevention, and to minimize student casualties, officers must be present on the premises full-time, ready to respond instantly. Support for this resource is essential, and our politicians must allocate funding for it; it is not optional.

3. Assign at least two full-time mental health counselors per 1,000 students for every school.

Rather than focusing solely on students with serious mental health issues, evidence suggests a more effective approach may involve identifying those who exhibit "red flag" behaviors that increase the likelihood of committing gun violence or acting out violently. Each year, mass shootings committed by individuals with serious mental illness account for less than 1% of all gun-related homicides, according to Dr. James Knoll and Dr. George Annas's report *Mass Shootings and Mental Illness*.[10] Ironically, individuals with mental illness are ten times more likely to become victims of violent crime than the general population.[11] *The Ultimate U.S. School Shooting Reference Guide, Volumes 1–3*, reinforces this data, showing that only 1.2% of the 1,204 reported school shootings stemmed from mental illness. Yet, following school shootings, politics and media often amplify this widespread misconception.

The benefit of having two full-time mental health counselors at each school is not only to help identify students with serious mental health issues, but to also assist students with anxiety, substance abuse issues, thoughts of suicide, and family issues.[12] Counselors help provide support for parents as well as teachers in order to help students become successful in their academics, as well as address student social and emotional needs. The administrative demands placed upon these professionals should be eased in order for counselors to be able to effectively provide adequate attention to developing student-counselor relationships, including being a critical part of a threat assessment team in order to prevent potential school shootings and violence in general.

4. Threat assessment and intervention teams.

Borrow strategies from the *Sandy Hook Promise "Safety Assessment & Intervention Training"* program. Developed by forensic clinical psychologist, Dewey G. Cornell, Ph.D, this national evidence-based violence prevention-program exists in over 1,000 schools in the United States.[13] This strategy involves:
 • Learning to identify threats;
 • Determining the seriousness of the threat, and;
 • Developing intervention plans in order to protect potential victims.

Insist that your school board and the Department of Education financially support this program every year, making school safety a priority. The best way to address school violence is to prevent it from happening in the first place and not take the success of the program for granted in following years. In order to get this program started in your own school, go to SandyHookPromise.org to learn more.

Following the attack at Columbine High School in 1999, U.S. Secret Service and U.S. Department of Education created a study report known as the *Safe School Initiative* in order to answer two queries: "Could we have known that these attacks were being planned?" and "What can be done to prevent future attacks from occurring?"[14] Similar to the Sandy Hook Promise, these departments concluded using a threat assessment approach in order to help prevent school-based attacks as the most effective approach. Most school shooters featured in this book and in *The Ultimate U.S. School Shooting Reference Guide, Volumes 1-3* either planned their attacks in advance; leaked their intentions to one or more of their peers; wrote about it in a journal or online platform; and/or were already of some concern to the people in their lives.

5. Focus on improving relationships between students, school resource officers (SROs), teachers, parents, and other school faculty.

CBS News reported that 17-year old Jamie Rouse told five friends about the shooting before it took place at Richland High School in 1995. One friend drove the shooter to school on the morning of the attack. "He saw that I had the gun," recalled Rouse. "I remember him making some, a comment like, 'So, you're really going to do it, aren't you?'" Rouse said, 'I guess I wanted someone to stop me.'"[15] If someone confesses about a shooting they want to commit, it is very possible that they are asking for help and hoping that you will stop them from acting on the threat. This is so important, that it bears repeating again and again–take every threat seriously! Speaking up saves lives!

Officers, teachers, and coaches are role models on campus, especially for troubled youth. These leaders are on the front lines of this ongoing battle, and they are the most underrated and unsung heroes who deserve our support. Students are the greatest source of intelligence when it comes to preventing any violence in schools. There are a disproportionate amount of school shootings in which other students have prior knowledge of the events weeks, days, and sometimes only minutes before the violence occurs. Unfortunately, students often do not alert an adult in order to prevent the tragedy. As a result, stronger bonds of trust are needed between adults and students, so that children feel comfortable and safe enough to speak up and help save lives.

If you're looking for books that can help strengthen relationships between school faculty and students, consider these insightful reads: *Culturize: Every Student. Every Day. Whatever It Takes* by Jimmy Casas and *Every Connection Matters: How to Build, Maintain, and Restore Relationships Inside the Classroom and Out* by Michael and Nita Creekmore.

6. Monitor your children's journals, phones, class assignments, and online activity.

Investigations into the Columbine mass school shooting revealed that the two perpetrators, Eric Harris and Dylan Klebold, had been planning together for over a year before their attack.[16] They documented their intentions in journals, wrote a class paper discussing a Columbine-like attack, and even produced a video using school equipment to act out killing scenes with weapons similar to those used in the actual shooting.[17]

In another tragic case from 2018, 13-year-old Keith M. Simons of Jackson Memorial Middle School expressed admiration for the Columbine shooters, declaring that he wanted his planned attack to "be bigger than anything this country's ever seen." Using the memo function on his cell phone, he outlined an eight-step plan for the assault.[18] For weeks, he prepared for the attack, but on the day he brought a shotgun to school, he changed his mind and took his own life in the bathroom instead.[19] Investigators later discovered a note he had written, which read: "When they interview my parents and ask how they didn't see the signs, they should know it's not them, it's me, and it's because of how I see the world."

Perhaps using a reputable phone monitoring app could help prevent similar tragedies in the future. I had the privilege of interviewing Clayton Cranford, a former school resource officer and the author of the book *Parenting in the Digital World.* For parents whose children have smartphones and tablets, he recommends using an app like OurPact to monitor online activity and ensure safety for both teenagers and younger children. Some "old-school" parents might argue that children don't have a right to privacy until they pay their own bills and live independently. Ultimately, however, the decision on setting privacy boundaries rests with parents or legal guardians.

For parents looking to guide their children through the digital world while ensuring online safety, these books offer valuable insights: *Raising Humans in a Digital World: Helping Kids Build a Healthy Relationship with Technology* by Diana Graber and *Screenwise: Helping Kids Thrive (and Survive) in Their Digital World* by Devorah Heitner.

7. Hire local community residents to be trained volunteer security forces at schools.

On February 1, 2018, a semi-automatic handgun accidentally discharged inside a 12-year-old girl's backpack in a science classroom at Salvador B. Castro Middle School in Los Angeles, injuring four students and a teacher.[20] The girl was arrested about 25 minutes after the incident. Despite the school having metal detecting wands, the shooter was not checked that day due to inconsistent use of the devices.[21] This highlights a critical issue: without consistent enforcement, the presence of metal detectors alone cannot effectively prevent gun violence in schools.

Even with regular use of metal detectors, their effectiveness is compromised if students can easily bypass them via access to unattended entrances. On January 15, 2002, at Martin Luther King, Jr. High School in New York City, seventeen-year-old Vincent Rodriguez entered through an unattended side door on 66th Street and hid a .380-caliber handgun in a fire extinguisher box on the fifth floor.[22] Later that day, Rodriguez shot and injured two students, Andre Wilkins and Andrel Napper, in a hallway, claiming they had teased his girlfriend.[23][24]

These incidents underscore the need for comprehensive security measures. Metal detectors must be used consistently, and all school entrances must be monitored. Many schools lack sufficient staff to conduct these checks. Hiring local community members, with proper background checks, to assist on a voluntary or minimum wage basis, could deter potential shooters and provide additional support for school resource officers. This approach not only enhances school safety, but also creates job opportunities within the community. These carefully vetted volunteers could also operate metal detectors and monitor entry points, allowing teachers to focus on their primary responsibilities of education.

8. Leverage and adapt existing community-based models used in order to help prevent violent extremism.

Adapting existing community-based models to prevent school gun violence offers significant advantages over creating new ones. These models have proven effectiveness, saving time and resources while leveraging established community trust. Their scalability allows for successful strategies to be replicated, creating safer school environments more efficiently. Overall, leveraging these tested models allows for immediate, cost-effective, and impactful action to be taken against school gun violence. Here are a few examples:

• Big Brothers Big Sisters of America (BBBSA) community-based mentoring programs.
• Department of Justice's "Comprehensive Gang Model."[25]
• Departments of Justice and Homeland Security "Building Communities of Trust" (BCOT) Initiative.[26]
• Departments of Education, Justice, and Health and Human Services "Safe Schools/Healthy Students" (SS/HS) Initiative.[27]

9. Designate a responsible gun-sitter.

On January 15, 2013, a domestic dispute between two young adults in Hazard, Kentucky, potentially over the custody of their shared child, tragically led to the fatal shooting of Caitlin Paige Cornett, age 20, her uncle Jackie Doug Cornett, age 53, and her cousin Taylor Cornett, age 12.[28] During a court-ordered visit, Dalton Lee Stidham (also known as Dalton Miller), age 21, met Caitlin in a parking lot at Hazard Community and Technical College to return their 2-year-old son.[29] It was there that he shot her and two members of her family. The owner of H&K Gun & Pawn Shop in Perry County reported that the suspect had purchased the gun from his shop about five hours before the shootings.[30] Perhaps if Stidham had sought help from a friend or family member to cool down and entrusted someone to temporarily hold his firearms, this tragic incident could have been avoided. Their two-year-old child might still have had the benefit of having both parents active in his life, instead of being abandoned to the foster system.

Whenever groups of friends go out to a bar or club, it is common sense for a designated driver to take their friends' keys. This prevents them from driving while intoxicated, which could result in harm to themselves or others. This behavior is a sign of maturity and responsibility. Similarly, if we notice a loved one going through an emotionally difficult situation, such as a domestic hardship, and they seem noticeably depressed, our concern for that person should extend to their safety. This includes insisting on "gun-sitting" and safely securing their firearms until the depression or difficult situation has passed.

Many instances in *The Ultimate U.S. School Shooting Reference Guide, Volumes 1-3* feature adults facing marital and child custody issues, workplace conflicts, or the loss of a loved one. Any of these powerful triggers can lead to disastrous results, including documented cases of school shootings. Gun-sitting a friend's or family member's firearms is a much preferable solution to having law enforcement resolve acts of gun violence that could permanently destroy a person's life. A mature and responsible alternative is to voluntarily turn in firearms to local law enforcement temporarily and seek professional help during difficult times.

10. Prevent gun theft by storing firearms in a locked gun safe.
On May 20, 1998, 15-year old Kip Kinkel was arrested for possessing a firearm in school. When Kip was returned home, he was afraid of his parent's reaction to his arrest. While his father was drinking coffee in the kitchen, Kip took a .22 rifle his father had bought for him; grabbed ammunition from his parents' bedroom, and shot his father in the back of the head.[31] After dragging his father's body to the bathroom, he waited for his mother to return home, then told her he

loved her, shot her in the back of the head twice, then three times in the face, and once in the heart.[32] The following day, Kip took 3 firearms, a hunting knife, and 1,127 rounds of ammunition with him to his school,[33] killing two students and injuring 25 others.

Between 2013 and 2015, a study conducted by Everytown for Gun Safety Support Fund still found that over half of the shooters obtained the gun used in the attack from their home, "likely because an adult did not store it locked and unloaded."[34] According to my research, 505 (or 40.2%) of all school shooting suspects were under the age of 18-years-old. This means they were too young to purchase a gun. This means that they either obtained the weapon from home, stole it from somewhere outside their home, or purchased it illegally on the streets. If you own firearms, please use a combination or key lock that no one else has access to, especially your children. This small safety measure may be an added expense for law-abiding gun owners, but it is an absolute necessity in order to prevent having your firearm used in a violent crime; including having your own firearm used against you or an innocent child.

11. Prevent gun theft by not announcing when you are going on vacation.

This helpful tip is for the entire family. Many proud and law-abiding gun owners will post images and videos of themselves on social media, using their firearms out on a shooting range or hunting trip, etc. These same individuals and/or their family members will often announce when and where they are going on vacation on their personal social media pages. Some may even post live videos of their vacation from their cell phone, hundreds or even thousands of miles away from their home. This is an invitation for any potential thief to get a five-finger discount on your guns at home. It is highly recommended that you wait until after you have returned from your vacation in order to share all about your exciting trip on social media. If your vacation is a predictable annual event, do not mention that you go every year. Any patient thief will just wait until next year to invade your home.

12. Prevent gun theft any time you are away from home.

On March 24, 1998, 13-year old Mitchell Scott Johnson and 11-year old Andrew Douglas Golden stole a van from Johnson's house, broke into Golden's grandfather's house, and stole high-powered rifles, pistols, and knives.[35] Afterward, the two boys drove to their school, triggered the fire alarm, and waited 100 yards away in the nearby woods for everyone to exit the buildings.[36] Once their fellow classmates and teachers gathered outside, Johnson and Golden opened fire, killing four students and one teacher, as well as injuring 10 others.

It is absolutely necessary to take every precaution to prevent break-ins every time you are away from home, even if you are just going out for a quick errand. Lock the deadbolt on your door at all times. Close and lock all windows and sliding glass doors when you are away, even if you live on the second floor. When I was a teenager, my friends and I liked to challenge our parkour skills and upper body strength for fun. Within less than 15 seconds, we were able to run up a wall and pull ourselves up to a friend's second floor balcony. Imagine if these skills were performed by someone with the intention of stealing unlocked firearms and your second floor balcony was left unlocked.

When you are away from home, consider keeping your window blinds closed, particularly at night because it makes it easy for anyone to view the contents of your home from the outside. Do not hide your key in an obvious location, such as on the door frame, under the doormat, or under a potted plant next to the door. Consider purchasing timers at a local hardware store and connect them to your lamps, radios, and/or televisions so that they turn on at random hours. If you work long or late hours, a cheap alternative to preventing home theft is to leave the kitchen or living room light on, as well as the television in the living room. Make the TV loud enough so that you can hear it just outside your front door, but not so loud that it will upset your neighbors. As a single parent working a full-time job and going to college in-person part-time, my mother used this simple security technique when I was a teenager. For extra measure, she would play a channel that featured vigorous religious preaching. This is intended to make any potential thief think someone is home and remind them, "God is always watching." In addition, never under-estimate the intimidation value of a good old-fashioned guard dog in the house, preferably one with a deep growl and low-pitched bark.

13. Prevent gun theft any time you are away from your vehicle and keep firearms secured and out of reach when children are left inside.

On May 21, 2018, reports revealed that Kenya Sandifer, a licensed gun owner, went to a school awards ceremony with her friend, Shameka Blackmon, her friend's sister, and a child—the latter two of which have special needs.[37] Before entering the school, reports indicated Sandifer allegedly left her gun unsecured in the back seat of the car. Once the group returned from the awards ceremony, the child picked up the gun and accidentally fired a shot into Blackmon's back.[38]

Another example involved a Greenville, South Carolina County Sheriff deputy's unlocked patrol car on November 12, 2018 at 4:15AM.[39] Two individuals were able to easily access the deputy's vehicle and stole his M-4 rifle, a .38 revolver, four magazines of bullets, and the deputy's body armor. Fortunately, one of the suspects was arrested and the rifle and body armor were retrieved. However, the pistol was never recovered. This gives the other suspect the potential to either illegally sell the deputy's weapon or commit a crime without having the weapon traced back to the suspect.

This safety precaution cannot be emphasized enough. If you have a license to carry your firearm with you, but have to leave it in your car for any reason, such as visiting a gun-free zone (i.e. schools, public libraries, federal buildings, airports, military bases, pawn shops, etc.), please take necessary precautions in order to prevent gun theft. Roll up your windows and lock all the doors of your vehicle at all times-unless there is a pet or small child in the vehicle, of course. If possible, lock your firearm in the glove compartment, trunk, or in a safe that is bolted to the floorboard or trunk of your vehicle.

14. Prevent theft, child access, suicides and accidental shootings by using key or combination firearm safes only accessible to authorized users.

On September 13, 2017, 15-year-old Caleb Sharpe accessed his father's gun safe using the combination he had learned. Inside, he found an AR-15 semi-automatic rifle and a .32-caliber handgun.[40] After leaving a suicide note for his parents, Sharpe concealed the weapons in a black duffle bag and brought them onto his school bus.[41] Upon arriving at school, he made his way to a second-floor hallway, where he attempted to load the AR-15. When the rifle jammed, a classmate approached him and said, chillingly, "I always knew you were going to shoot up the school."[42] In response, Sharpe pulled out the .32-caliber handgun, shooting the 15-year-old student first in the abdomen and then fatally in the face.[43]

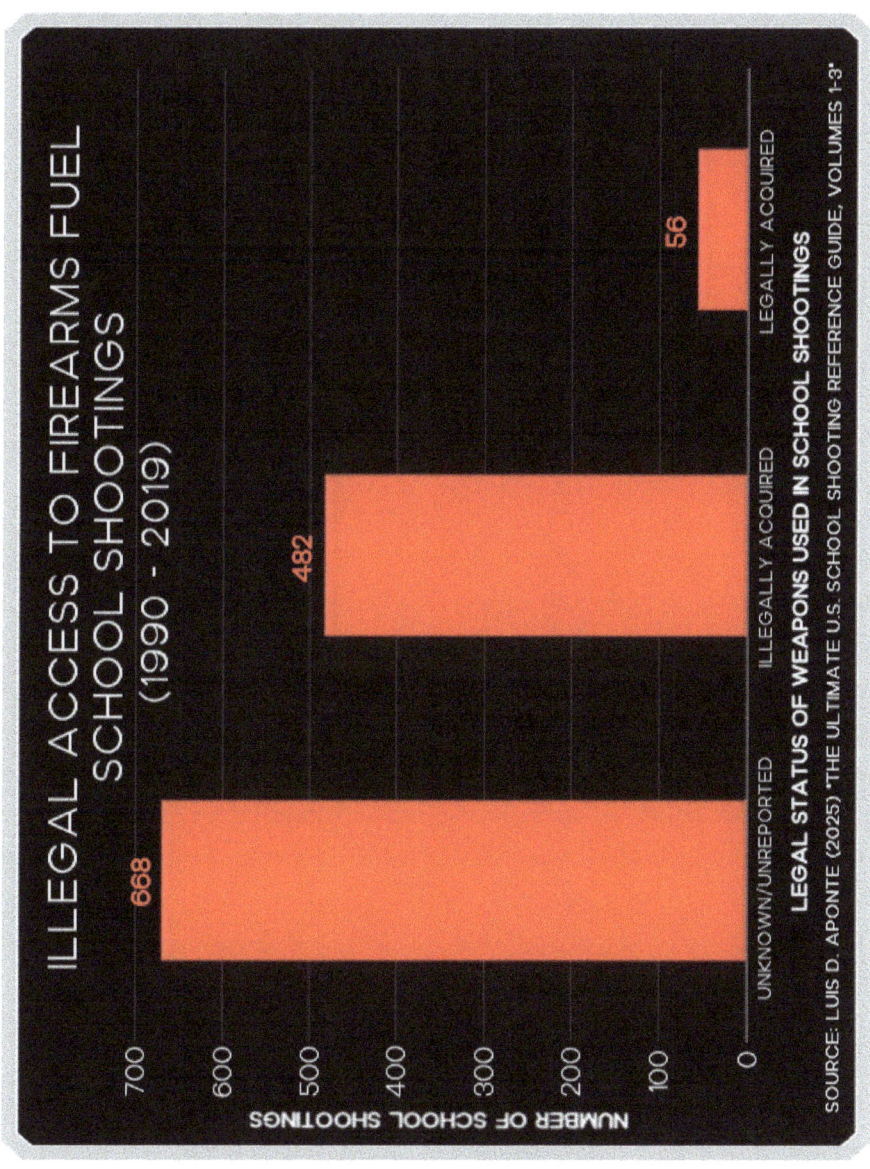

Illegal access to firearms fuel school shootings (1990-2019).
Infographic created by Luis D. Aponte. Based on "The Ultimate U.S. School Shooting Reference Guide, Volumes 1-3" by Luis D. Aponte.

If you have guns at home, storing them safely and securely is absolutely crucial to keep them out of the wrong hands. Out of 1,204 U.S. school shootings, at least 482 (or 40%) involved firearms that were obtained illegally. Gun experts—including many gun owners—define "safe" as ensuring firearms are always unloaded, while "secure" means locking them in a gun safe with a key or combination that unauthorized individuals—like children—cannot access. Safe storage reduces accidental discharges, while secure storage prevents unauthorized access. Some gun owners worry that these precautions might delay access during emergencies, leading them to favor biometric gun locks that open with a thumbprint—quick and convenient, right? But unfortunately, things don't always go as planned. Between January 2019 and October 2023, over 120,000 biometric locks sold by major retailers such as Walmart, Amazon, and Bass Pro Shops were recalled due to malfunctions.[44] These faulty locks allowed anyone to open them, tragically resulting in incidents like the death of a 12-year-old boy.[45] This is a chilling scenario for any parent or gun owner. Fortunately, advances in quick-access gun safes (excluding the flawed biometric models) offer a viable solution, balancing speed with security. The peace of mind that comes from knowing children cannot access firearms far outweighs the seconds potentially saved in emergencies. Consistently practicing safe and secure firearm storage could make all the difference, helping prevent tragedies like Caleb Sharpe gaining access to his father's guns.

15. Check your firearms daily.

On October 21, 2013, the parents of 12-year-old Jose Reyes didn't realize their son had taken their 9mm Ruger handgun, which had been carelessly left in an unlocked case on top of the refrigerator.[46] On a single page of a spiral notebook, Reyes wrote that he was taunted as being gay, lazy, stupid, an idiot, as well as had his money stolen, and was accused of wetting his pants.[47] In response, Reyes reportedly took the gun to his middle school, fatally shot math teacher and former

U.S. Marine Mike Landsberry, wounded two fellow students, and then ended his own life.[48]

A 2004 report by the U.S. Secret Service and the Department of Education revealed that 68% of school shooters obtained their firearms from their own home or a relative.[49] If you're a responsible gun owner who takes pride in securing your firearms, remember: even the best-hidden guns can be stolen. It's not enough to lock them away—you need to check daily to ensure your firearms are exactly where they should be. "Safe" and "secure" means more than just keeping them out of sight. It doesn't mean stashing them in a sock drawer, the secret pocket of your purse, under your pillow, on the entertainment stand, atop the refrigerator, in a shoebox under the bed, or visibly mounted on a truck's overhead gun rack. True safety requires a secure gun safe and the diligence to double-check its contents regularly. This small habit doesn't demand an act of Congress but it could save lives. As detailed in *The Ultimate U.S. School Shooting Reference Guide, Volumes 1–3*, many school shooters obtained their firearms from a parent, grandparent, friend, or neighbor. Tragically, parents often express shock, realizing too late that their guns were missing.

16. Be a true friend, not an agitator.

Fifteen-year-old Charles Andrew "Andy" Williams Jr., "a good Christian from Maryland,"[50] confided in at least a dozen fellow students about his plan to bring a gun to school and "pull a Columbine."[51] Two of his friends called him a "p***y" and dared him to do it.[52] Williams also told friends in Maryland that he was contemplating suicide. On March 5, 2001, Williams stole a German Arminius .22-caliber revolver and 40 bullets from his father's locked gun collection, went to Santana High School in Santee, California, and killed 2 people and injured 13 more in a school bathroom and adjacent courtyard.[53] Most of his victims were teenaged students who Williams claimed had bullied him.[54] Williams was apprehended by police officers approximately six minutes after the shooting began.

When someone shows signs of stress, depression, anxiety, or rage, combined with threats of bringing a gun to school or committing suicide, ignoring or enabling such behavior can have life-altering consequences—including risking your own safety. Being a true friend, rather than an agitator, can save lives—potentially those of the people you care about most. It's easy to condemn a shooter's act of terror—until it happens at your school. Then, the regret of staying silent, or daring them carry out the tragic act, knowing you could have spoken up and helped that person get the support they desperately needed, can be overwhelming. Take every threat seriously. Students are on the front lines of this ever-present danger infiltrating schools nationwide. While school resource officers and staff play a critical role in prevention, they can't act alone. Brave students must step up, take responsibility, and be part of the solution by speaking out.

One of my favorite books for building strong relationships is *How to Win Friends & Influence People* by Dale Carnegie. I've read it at least three times because its insights are timeless, and it's an enjoyable, thought-provoking read. Another great recommendation for fostering and maintaining friendships is *Big Friendship: How We Keep Each Other Close* by Aminatou Sow.

17. *Be Nice* campaigns.

Sixteen-year-old Evan Ramsey had a childhood marked by hardship. With his father in prison and his mother battling alcoholism, he also endured abuse in foster homes.[55] At school, he faced relentless teasing and bullying, potentially fueling a sense of rage, rejection, and vulnerability. Ramsey, along with two friends, planned a shooting and even hinted at their intentions to other students. Despite telling one girl he intended to bring a shotgun to school, no one alerted an adult.[56] On February 19, 1997, Ramsey walked into Bethel Regional High School in Bethel, Alaska, with a 12-gauge shotgun that he had stolen from his legal guardian's home. Just before the opening bell, he shot at his former girlfriend,[57] killed school principal Ronald Dale Edwards, age 50, and fellow classmate Joshua Palacios, age 16, and injured two other students, Shane McIntyre and Russell Lamont. Ramsey then placed the shotgun under his chin, intending to commit suicide, but ultimately surrendered to law enforcement.[58]

Every person has a unique story, filled with unseen struggles. Sometimes, a simple smile or a small act of kindness can light up someone's day in ways you might never imagine. If you are a student, consider taking the initiative to walk up to a fellow classmate who sits alone, simply smile, and say, "Hello." Invite a classmate who normally doesn't have a voluntary partner and offer to be theirs. Thank your teachers, coaches, and resource officers for all the hard work they do because they battle with hardships as well. Walk up to someone you don't know and find something simple to genuinely compliment about them. As role models, this is a critically important virtue for adults to display, especially toward children and young adults. Make an effort to show interest in someone who may be struggling with their own challenges. If you are concerned about your personal safety, do it as a group or ask for help from a professional–such as a counselor, police officer, teacher, or an influential relative. A small act of kindness at the right time may have a huge, long-term impact on someone who needs it the most at that exact moment. Someone's world may be falling apart, and a kind word or nonjudgmental ear from a friend may help heal their anguish. Kindness can save a life.

This heroic virtue of kindness is especially important online. It takes only a few seconds of your time to say something positive and uplifting to someone. Such small acts can make a tremendous impact on someone struggling in an emotionally dark place. Conversely, internet trolls can cause significant emotional distress by spreading harmful words that are magnified online for all to see. We need more everyday heroes looking out for each other, regardless of our differences. For more information about starting a bullying prevention program at your child's school, go to StandForTheSilent.org.

18. See something? For everyone's sake, say something!

Always take shooting and suicide threats seriously. On March 20, 2017, the Frederick County Sheriff's Office in Maryland reported they were able to prevent another mass school shooting because the father of 18-year-old Nicole Cevario spoke up and warned Catoctin High School in Maryland about a potential threat of violence towards the school.[59] [60] Cevario allegedly possessed a legally-purchased shotgun and materials for making a pipe bomb. In Cevario's diary, detectives discovered information about her school's emergency procedures and references to mistakes made in both the Columbine, Colorado and Newton, Connecticut mass shootings.[61] She planned to attack the school on April 5, 2017 and intended to die during the attack.[62]

Another courageous story comes from a mother in College Place, Washington in October 2019. A woman named Nichole turned in her 17-year old son to the police when she discovered a detailed plan in his journal to attack his school on April 20, 2020–the anniversary of the Columbine school shooting. Terrifying details in the journal included plans to detonate pipe bombs and use multiple firearms to "blast anyone in sight" and "execute survivors."[63] Although the mother felt guilty that perhaps she had done something wrong, potentially dozens of innocent lives were saved thanks to the courage of both of these brave and responsible parents. In the aftermath of a school shooting, parents were often surprised that their child had any weapon in their possession before they committed the violent act. If at any time you suspect your child may be in possession of a firearm without your consent or knowledge, please notify law enforcement to intervene preemptively before they potentially take another person's life and perhaps their own. In most examples of school gun violence, the shooter is afraid of facing the consequences of their actions and often commit suicide within seconds after their attack. It is better to intervene early and allow children to get the professional help they need.

Most police departments have a tip hotline where you can report a potential school shooting or suicide attempt. Locate that number now and save it in your cell phone contacts. If the threat is imminent, immediately call 911 and then notify your teacher, principle, parents, etc. Several suspects featured in *The Ultimate U.S. School Shooting Reference Guide, Volumes 1-3* told a fellow classmate, friend, family member, or posted on an online forum about their intention to shoot up a school at least a day or so before it happened. Too many people don't take the threat seriously enough or are afraid to be labeled as a "snitch." Reports revealed that some children have even encouraged or dared their fellow classmate to carry out the shooting. Staying silent means people die. The earlier a threat can be identified, reported, and intercepted, the more likely a deadly shooting can be prevented. Even if the threat comes from a family member or friend, online or in person, you never know how many lives you might be saving by having the courage to speak up, including your own.

Do not assume that you are safe by remaining quiet, just because the person is your friend or family member. On March 2, 2018, the night before the shooting, 19-year old James David, Jr., approached Central Michigan University campus officers expressing vague concerns that someone was out to hurt him.[64] A few hours later, Davis admitted he was under the influence of drugs and was treated in a hospital that night.[65] His parents, including his father, who was a police officer, picked Davis up from the hospital the following morning and helped him get his belongings from his college dorm room. That is when Davis Jr. took his father's gun from the family vehicle, returned to his campus room, and killed both of his parents.

Shooters often report that they felt emotionally numb during a school attack and may not realize who they have killed or injured until after the carnage is over. This is why it is extremely important to say something if you see or hear something as soon as possible. Please do not hesitate to save lives.

19. Seek professional help and a positive support group.

On April 2, 2012, forty-three-year-old One L. Goh, also known as Su Nam Ko, a former student at Oikos University–a small Christian college–opened fire in the middle of a classroom with a .45-caliber semi-automatic handgun, leaving seven dead and three injured in Oakland, California.[66][67] Oakland Police Chief Howard Jordan stated, "They laughed at him. They made fun of his lack of English-speaking skills. It made him feel isolated..."[68] Two court-appointed psychiatrists determined that Goh suffered from paranoid schizophrenia.[69] June Lee, executive director of the Korean Community Center of the East Bay, said, "The community had no awareness of how to deal with it. They find it really horrifying. In the Korean community, if you have cancer, people will talk about it. But if you have mental illness, nobody wants to talk about it."[70]

Whether you, a loved one, or an acquaintance struggles with emotional or mental health issues, have the courage to seek professional help. Recognizing when you or someone you love needs support takes courage, and accepting that help takes even greater strength. If you're facing challenges like depression, bullying, rejection, relationship issues, divorce, school or work difficulties, or financial problems, professional counseling or therapy can be a lifesaver.

Start by visiting your local public library. They can provide contact information for emergency mental health, substance use disorder, and other resources. You are not alone. It's worth repeating: there are people who care about you and would be devastated to lose you. You are not alone!

One of my oldest and closest friends recently went through a difficult divorce and had to deal with the fact that his wife was unfaithful. They have children together and were married for 15 years. He owns several guns, but thankfully, my friend had the forethought and self-control to ask his adult brother to lock away his guns until he received professional help and had at least a year to process his grief.

The tremendous stress of losing his wife and not being able to see his children caused him to lose over 50 pounds in less than five months. His siblings and I begged him to seek help because he was having suicidal thoughts. He admitted that he was ashamed to see a counselor because of his pride as a man and the perceived stigma surrounding it. However, afterward, he told me that he actually enjoyed the therapy sessions and that they may have saved his life. Speaking with a counselor felt as though a heavy weight from his chest was beginning to lift.

There is no shame in sharing your problems with a professional who may be able to help. This stigma is often internalized due to misguided pride and a toxic macho culture. You may not feel that anyone cares during your darkest hour, but there are people who love you and truly want to help. Many people have been in similar situations and can help you through this difficult journey. Talk with your primary care doctor, a family counselor, a school counselor, a trusted religious clergy member, family members, or a close friend who may be able to help. Again, if you do not know where to begin, visit your local public library and ask a librarian about social services available in your area. Overcoming personal struggles and trauma is never easy, but having a dependable support group can make all the difference in the world. All you have to do is be open and willing to reach out for—and accept—help. You can and will get through this difficult time and become stronger. Be patient and give the process as much time as you need. Surround yourself with positive and supportive people. Let go of anyone who drains light from your life.

If you're facing emotional or mental health challenges, these two books might be particularly helpful: *The Body Keeps the Score: Brain, Mind, and Body in the Healing of Trauma* by Bessel van der Kolk, M.D., and *The Happiness Trap* by Russ Harris.

20. Enhance security by increasing police and volunteer presence at school games, extracurricular events, and dismissal times, and encourage witness cooperation with law enforcement.

Out of 1,204 U.S. school shootings, 465 suspects (36.4%) were never apprehended by authorities. Often, law enforcement struggles to find the culprits responsible for these senseless attacks due to lack of security personnel, the unwillingness of witnesses to speak with police, insufficient lighting at night, and the absence of motion-activated outdoor cameras monitoring afterschool activities. For example, on December 8, 2017, in Champaign, Illinois, following a high school basketball game between the Danville High School Vikings and the Champaign Central Maroons, a shooting occurred around 9:20 p.m. As a large crowd moved outside the school after the game for "a potential fight," gunshots were fired, injuring three females aged 15, 17, and 18.[71] Despite the severity of the attack, more than two years later, no arrests had been made. The lack of police presence at the game and the reluctance of witnesses to provide information hindered the investigation.[72]

Several unsolved shootings have occurred in school parking lots during or immediately after evening games or extracurricular activities. These incidents often involve teens or adults whose arguments escalate into gun violence, allowing the perpetrators to escape before being identified. Additionally, several gang-related drive-by shootings have taken place in front of schools just as classes are dismissed, leaving students vulnerable. Increasing police and volunteer security presence in these areas, along with designating safe waiting zones, could be a simple yet effective solution to prevent such tragic incidents.

Adopting stronger school policies and passing legislation to mandate enhanced security measures in schools—such as mandatory security for afterschool activities, improved lighting, and the installation of security cameras—are critical steps. However, no policy or law will be as effective as strong community involvement in fostering a safer environment for children. Parents can join Parent Advisory Committees (PACs) to not only stay informed about their child's school, but also collaborate to encourage witness cooperation with law enforcement and educate local residents on the importance of reporting suspicious activities. This collective effort helps bridge the gap between police and the public, ultimately creating a more secure environment for everyone.

21. Encourage schools to host athletic events in the morning.

Imagine a world without the timeless tradition of school sports. This cherished practice offers more than just a means of exercise and burning off excess energy. It unleashes feel-good hormones, fosters friendships, and hones team-building and problem-solving skills. Most importantly, it's fun! For some underprivileged students, an athletic scholarship is a golden ticket, a chance to forge a new legacy for themselves and their family. It's a source of pride and symbolizes years of sacrifice for both the student and their parents, both financially and socially. For those with the discipline to reach elite status, the honor, pride, and excitement of representing their country on the world's biggest stage—the Olympics—await. Some may even secure multi-million-dollar professional contracts, turning their passion into a lucrative career.

Yet, without a community strategy to prevent school gun violence, these dreams can be snuffed out before they even begin. Out of at least 127 reported shootings at school sporting events, 115 (90.5%) occurred during or shortly after basketball and football games and practices. The remaining 12 (9.4%) were spread across track, baseball, soccer, and volleyball events. Given the timing of these tragedies, a simple preventive measure might be to host school games in the morning on weekends. Sixty-nine percent of these shootings happened in the evening, with 13.4% in the afternoon and only 0.7% in the morning. Unfortunately, the timing of 25.9% of these incidents remains unreported.

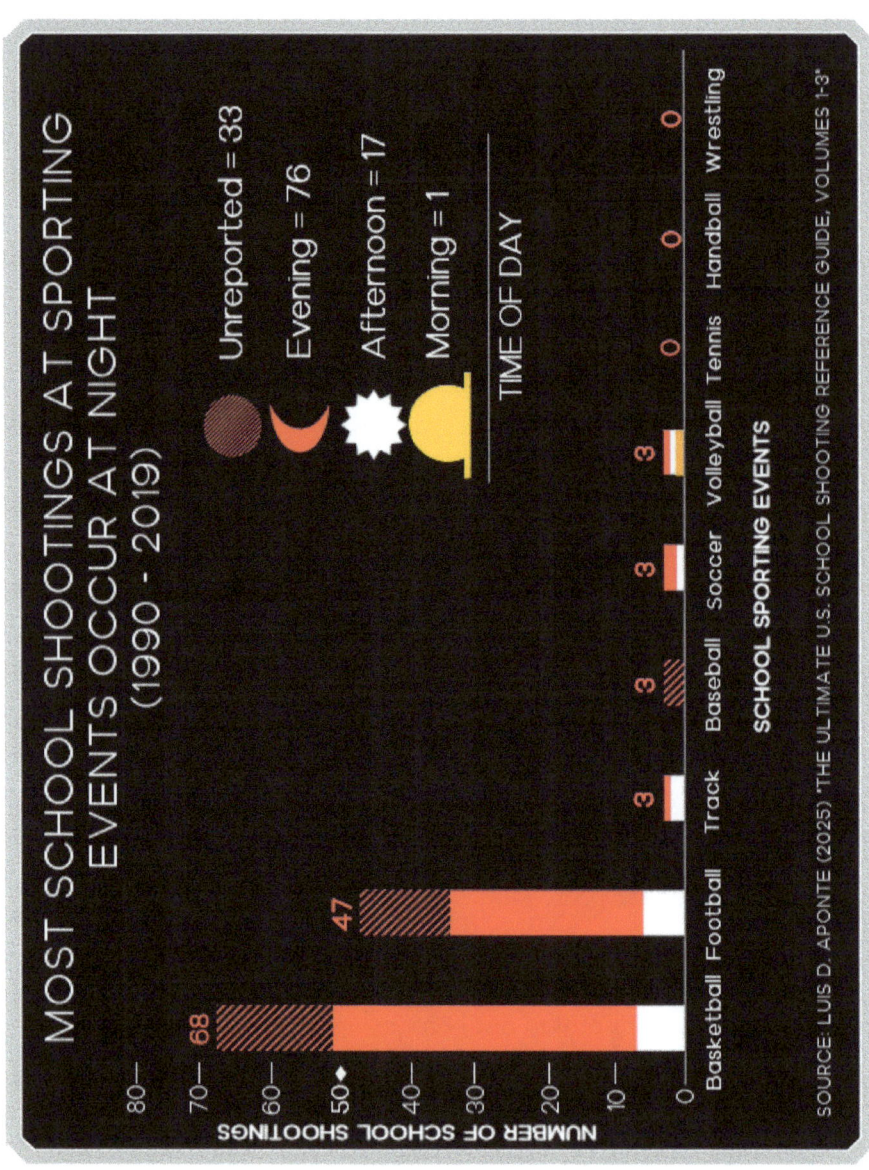

Most U.S. school shootings at sporting events occur at night (1990-2019).
Infographic created by Luis D. Aponte. Based on "The Ultimate U.S. School Shooting Reference Guide, Volumes 1-3" by Luis D. Aponte.

While it's unclear why basketball and football events appear to be more susceptible to school gun violence, it seems preventable. If schools are unwilling to change game times, an alternative might be to switch to a different sport that offers college scholarships and Olympic representation and still aligns with a child's aspirations.

22. Integrate consistent metal detector use with other safety measures.

The use of metal detectors in schools has long been a controversial topic in the realm of school safety. In 1990, Chicago Mayor Richard Daley introduced several measures to enhance school safety in response to escalating youth violence.[73] These measures included expanding police patrols in high schools and installing walk-through metal detectors in every city high school. Despite resistance to the latter, the first year saw 153 arrests for carrying guns and 380 arrests for carrying knives and other weapons.[74] The following year, the mayor's report documented the confiscation of 192 guns.[75] It's crucial to note that these actions were intended to address the specific security concerns of Chicago at the time and may not necessarily reflect the needs of all schools nationwide today.

The consistent use of walk-through metal detectors in Chicago high schools has clearly demonstrated its effectiveness in identifying and preventing weapons from entering schools. Combined with police patrols, this approach justifies the need for sustained, multi-faceted security measures. While such interventions can foster a sense of safety among students, parents, and staff, some may argue that they also create an environment of distrust. The challenge of relying solely on metal detectors and police is that it doesn't address the root causes of gun violence and violence in general within schools. A balanced approach would integrate metal detectors with other safety measures, such as comprehensive mental health support, anti-bullying initiatives, and community engagement programs. Ultimately, it's up to communities and schools to determine the menu of solutions that best serve their unique needs.

If a school opts to invest in hand-held or walk-through metal detectors, history suggests that consistent use is crucial. On November 20, 1992, fifteen-year-old Joseph White, a high school freshman with a criminal history of theft and gang violence, brought a gun to Edward Tilden High School in Chicago, resulting in the death of one student and the injury of two others over a gambling debt dispute.[76] Despite having metal detectors installed, the school principal admitted they were used only once per month due to staffing and operational costs.[77] This tragic incident underscores the security challenges of inconsistent metal detector use, while acknowledging that it's impossible to fully understand all the unique security challenges the school may have faced.

Some administrators argue that metal detectors may make a school appear to be a dangerous place. However, as a former TSA officer, I can attest that the daily use of metal detectors and x-ray machines ensures the safety of millions of airline travelers every day since the terrorist attacks on September 11, 2001. Anyone who has had the privilege of serving for jury duty has experienced security screening before entering the courthouse. The same is true for professional football and baseball games in multi-million-dollar stadiums. Securing the safety of children in schools should be just as important as protecting lawyers, tourists, and professional athletes. While the major challenges with daily metal detector use include the required staff, time, and money—especially in large schools—commitment to their daily use can help reduce the number of weapons entering schools. This effort can be supported by vetted community volunteers and approved students needing volunteer hours. Additionally, balancing metal detector use with comprehensive mental health support, anti-bullying initiatives, and community engagement programs will contribute to a safer school environment. This balanced perspective, supported by community involvement, can lead to more effective and accepted solutions based on each community's needs.

23. Suicide prevention programs at schools.

The tragic reality of suicide is a preventable aspect of school shootings that often goes unnoticed. Many of the deadliest incidents, such as those at Virginia Tech, Columbine, and Sandy Hook, ended in the shooter taking their own life. Out of 1,204 reported school shootings, at least 214 (17.7%) resulted in suicide or attempted suicide. Yet, national news rarely covers suicides that harm only the shooter. There are numerous instances where a student, having accessed a parent's gun, entered a school bathroom, classroom, or hallway and ended their life without harming others. To prevent such tragedies, multiple strategies must be considered.

On February 25, 1998, a 13-year-old boy smuggled a .22-caliber rifle into Reed City Middle School in Michigan, concealed in a guitar case.[78] His father had bought the rifle for hunting and target practice. "He was just standing there before school, laughing and joking with his friends," said Police Chief Bill Riemersma. "And when everyone went to their lockers, he just reached into his locker and shot himself."[79] Two days before the shooting, the boy told his friends that he wouldn't be around to see his birthday.[80] In September, reports indicated he had dictated his will to a friend, detailing how his belongings should be divided. This heartbreaking story underscores the importance of gun safety classes, secure firearm storage, taking suicide threats seriously, and establishing school suicide prevention programs.

If you're struggling with depression or seeking guidance on suicide prevention, these two books may offer valuable insight: *Reasons to Stay Alive* by Matt Haig and *Beneath the Surface: A Teen's Guide to Reaching Out When You or Your Friend Is in Crisis* by Kristi Hugstad.

24. Zero-tolerance policy for gang activity, behavior, or displaying of gang colors or clothing.

Out of 1,204 U.S. school shootings, at least 100 were reported as being gang-related. On December 12, 2014, as students gathered for their noon lunch break at Rosemary Anderson High School in Portland, Oregon, sixteen-year-old Marquise Murphy unleashed chaos with a 9mm Ruger handgun, wounding four individuals. He injured David Jackson-Lyday, age 20; Taylor Zimmer, age 16; LaBraye Franklin, age 17; and Olyvia Batson, age 17.[81] Murphy had no prior criminal history. However, two days before the shooting, he recorded a cellphone video showing himself waving the gun and warning a rival gang that "...it's war time, be ready and stay strapped because we coming with full clips."[82] Murphy's 22-year-old brother, Lonzo Murphy, and 18-year-old Marquel Dugas were also charged with attempted murder, assault, and unlawful use of a weapon.[83] Additionally, 19-year-old Geno Malique King was accused of trying to help Marquise Murphy flee the state by driving a car toward Las Vegas.[84] Police said one of the victims, David Jackson-Lyday, was a member of a rival gang.[85] This tragedy outlines the critical need for parents, schools, and community members to maintain a hard, zero-tolerance stance on gang-activity, gang-related behavior, or the displaying of gang colors.

Many of the 100 gang-related school shootings remain unsolved, with several suspects still at large, according to reports. Research from *The Ultimate U.S. School Shooting Reference Guide, Volumes 1-3* indicates that some conflicts escalate from perceived disrespect by a rival gang member; gambling on campus; wearing clothing associated with specific gangs; robbery of another student; or territorial disputes. Addressing this challenge requires a community effort in collaboration with local law enforcement to obtain centralized gang intelligence aimed at disrupting gang activity and preventing gun violence in schools. No community can afford to view this as someone else's problem, as school gun violence is prevalent in both large cities and small towns, in wealthy and impoverished areas, in public and private schools, and in both Democratic and Republican states.

25. Review and update school security protocols: prioritizing safety in schools.

Assuming that a school is safe from repeat attacks simply because it has already faced a shooting is a dangerous misconception. The proverb "Lightning never strikes the same place twice" may offer hope, but it falls short of reality when it comes to school gun violence.

Consider the story of Savannah State University in Savannah, Georgia, the city of my birth. Despite stepping up security measures in 2008, 2015, 2018, and 2019,[86][87][88][89] Savannah State University reported at least 11 shootings between 2008 and 2022. Alarmingly, the violence persisted with two individuals shot in 2022, on campus, at T.A. Wright Stadium.[90][91] Shockingly, reports indicate that nine of the shootings at Savannah State University occurred at the student housing apartments. For more information, see *The Ultimate U.S. School Shooting Reference Guide, Volumes 1-3*.

While it may seem unlikely for a school to endure multiple shootings, the grim reality is that at least 82 schools in the United States experienced two or more incidents between 1990 and 2019. Notably, even Harvard University faced such incidents in both 2009 and 2010.[92][93] Even more alarming, at least 10 schools endured four or more shootings during this period. These staggering statistics highlight the urgent need for proactive and preventative measures.

Enhancing security protocols on expansive university campuses can be resource-intensive, and skeptics may argue that such efforts might not yield significant results. Yet, inaction could carry devastating consequences for both students and staff. Furthermore, a lack of an appropriate response to such a threat may impact parents' willingness to enroll their children in a school they see as not taking security seriously.

The community must come together to determine the best solutions for its environment and culture. Remember, taking action now can prevent future tragedies. Below is a list of the top 25 schools in the U.S. that have experienced multiple shootings.

#. School Name, City, State: Number of Shootings

25. Battery Creek High School, Beaufort, SC: 2
24. Alabama A&M University, Huntsville, AL: 2
23. Agape Christian Academy (PreK - 12), Pine Hills, FL: 2
22. Wichita State University, Wichita, KS: 3
21. Voorhees College, Denmark, SC: 3
20. University of Utah, Salt Lake City, UT: 3
19. University of Akron, Akron, OH: 3
18. Skyline High School, Dallas, TX: 3
17. Robert E. Lee High School, Montgomery, AL: 3
16. Osborn High School, Detroit, MI: 3
15. Ohio State University, Columbus, OH: 3
14. Lane College, Jackson, TN: 3
13. Huffman High School, Birmingham, AL: 3
12. Elizabeth City State University, Elizabeth City, NC: 3
11. Arkansas State University, Jonesboro, AR: 3
10. Virginia State University, Petersburg, VA: 4
9. Virginia Commonwealth University, Richmond, VA: 4
8. Texas Southern University, Houston, TX: 4
7. Delaware State University, Dover, DE: 4
6. South Carolina State University, Orangeburg, SC: 5
5. Langston University, Langston, OK: 5
4. Tennessee State University, Nashville, TN: 6
3. Jackson State University, Jackson, MS: 7
2. Grambling State University, Grambling, LA: 8
1. Savannah State University, Savannah, GA: 10

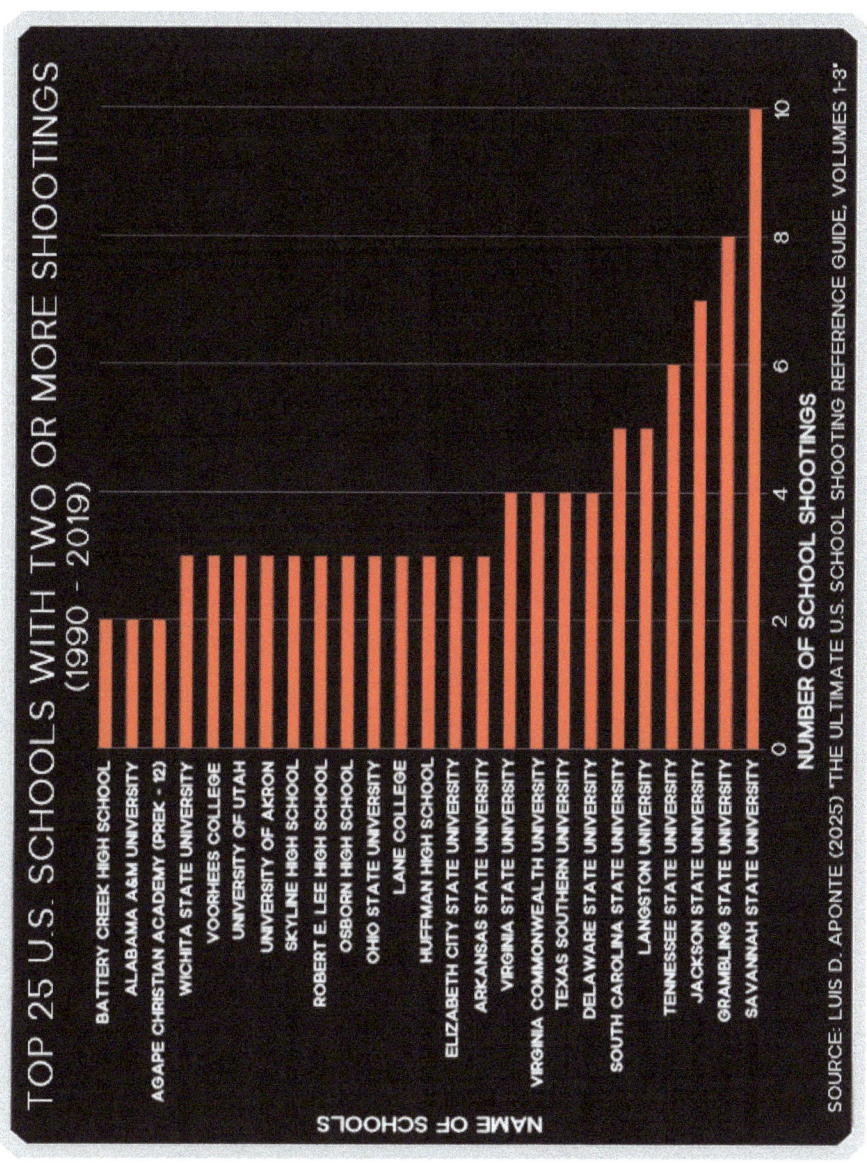

Top 25 U.S. schools with two or more shootings (1990-2019).
Infographic created by Luis D. Aponte. Based on "The Ultimate U.S. School Shooting Reference Guide, Volumes 1-3" by Luis D. Aponte.

26. Partner with Community Violence Intervention (CVI) programs.

Losing a loved one, especially to another person's actions, tests the very core of our spirit and values. Yet, within this pain, we must find the strength to rise above, to seek healing rather than revenge. It often takes the support of friends, family, and our community to navigate this dark journey. Ultimately, we hold on to the belief that our loved one's death can ignite a greater purpose, that justice will be served, and that we can and will be inspired to go on to live life with even more passion and purpose.

It is important to note that 442 (or 36.7%) of all U.S. school shootings from 1990-2019 stemmed from arguments, feuds, fights, and revenge. On January 9, 2009, 18-year-old Georgio Dukes wreaked havoc at Paul Lawrence Dunbar Vocational Career Academy High School in Chicago, Illinois, just as students were leaving a basketball game around 8:00 p.m.[94] He fired at least 18 bullets using .45-caliber and .40-caliber Winchester firearms, injuring five people: John Sharp, age 19; Jerome Sharp, age16; Deric Balark, age 18; Raymond Jefferson, age 18; and Shamari Smith, age 16.[95] Police suspected the shooting was gang-related; however, Dukes' mother denied her son was involved in gangs, noting he was a business student enrolled at Miles College near Birmingham, Alabama.[96] Court prosecutors argued that Georgio allegedly sought revenge for the murder of his twin brother, Sergio Dukes, on December 3, 2008—a motive the defendant denied.[97] Regardless of the true motivation that led a college student to fire 18 bullets at a group of people leaving a high school basketball game, a Community Violence Intervention program might have prevented such a tragedy and preserved a potentially bright future.

Community Violence Intervention (CVI) programs are evidence-based, community-centered initiatives designed to reduce violence through targeted, strategic efforts.[98] These programs employ credible messengers—individuals with lived experiences and hyperlocal community knowledge—to reach out to those at the highest risk of involvement in violence, and operate in places that police and other public safety workers generally cannot.[99] These messengers connect with and build trust among some of the hardest-to-reach individuals in violence-impacted communities. This trust and credibility enable them to mediate conflicts, prevent retaliation, and intervene in potentially violent situations before they escalate. Additionally, they collaborate with service providers, community stakeholders, government agencies, and system partners within a broader violence prevention ecosystem.

Evaluations of CVI programs have found that they have reduced shooting victimization in major U.S. cities, such as New York, by as much as 63%, and reduced retaliation killings by up to 85% in New Orleans and 100% in Chicago.[100] [101] Despite their remarkable success and proven track record, CVI programs have historically been underfunded. However, in 2022, the *Bipartisan Safer Communities Act* (BSCA) provided over $94 million in supplemental Community Violence Intervention and Prevention Initiative (CVIPI) grants.[102] This bipartisan effort has been instrumental in supporting these community-tailored programs that not only help disrupt the cycle of shootings, violence, and retaliation, but also help establish relationships between individuals and community assets to deliver services that save lives, address trauma, provide opportunities, and improve the physical, social, and economic conditions that drive violence.[103]

Search online to see if your state has dedicated funding to violence intervention programs and partner with these groups in your community. Visit the National CVIPI Resource Center to request training and technical assistance from CVI experts at www.lisc.org. There is also a step-by-step checklist for community-led and evidence-informed strategies via the U.S. Department of Justice Office of Justice Programs titled "CVI Implementation Checklist."[104] This checklist is also available on my website as a free downloadable PDF titled "Community-Based Violence Intervention & Prevention Checklist" at ASafePlaceBook.com/resources.

With countless variables and patterns to consider, one thing is clear: there's no single solution to preventing the next school shooting. Every community must figure out which strategies work best for them, relying on evidence-based approaches. Creating a truly safe school environment requires students, parents, educators, and community leaders to come together with a comprehensive plan that intertwines emotional mastery, mental health support, updated security measures, community involvement, and other proactive interventions.

Research from *The Ultimate U.S. School Shooting Reference Guide, Volumes 1-3* reveals that fights, feuds, and arguments are the leading causes of most school shootings. This highlights the critical need to teach children and young adults essential social skills, like conflict resolution, de-escalation techniques, and emotional mastery. These skills not only nurture healthy social development but may also lower the risk of violence. Many young people who feel the need to bring weapons to school cite concerns about their own safety. Additionally, most school shootings involve individuals aged 13 to 25—a pivotal period when adolescents are navigating the transition to adulthood.

Considering these factors, introducing martial arts training at an early age could be a game changer for fostering self-confidence and emotional control. Since many, if not most, physical fights end up on the ground, Brazilian Jiu-Jitsu is an excellent option. For self-defense against multiple attackers, Krav Maga or Muay Thai (Thai boxing) stand out as being particularly effective. However, it's crucial to understand that learning martial arts brings with it a moral and legal obligation to use such skills responsibly. There's always a chance that children or teens could misuse this knowledge, which is why finding instructors who stress emotional mastery and ethical principles is so important.

Statistics show that most school shootings happen outdoors, especially in K-12 parking lots or around university dormitories. To boost safety, schools might consider hiring at least one trained and armed security officer per 1,000 students, as well as organizing vetted community volunteers to oversee vulnerable outdoor spaces. School resource officers can play an essential role by building positive connections with students, especially those who may have concerns about law enforcement's role in a school setting. Additionally, schools should strive to provide at least two mental health counselors per 1,000 students, ensuring these professionals are accessible to those who need them most—rather than buried in administrative work. Reducing the stigma around seeking mental health support is vital so that students feel encouraged to reach out for help.

Understandably, budget limitations often pose challenges for school administrations and taxpayers. Some districts may not be able to afford additional resource officers or counselors. However, creative solutions, such as applying for federal and state grants, hosting community fundraisers, partnering with local businesses or nonprofits, and mobilizing parents and educators to advocate for increased funding, can make a significant difference.

Parents play a pivotal role, too, by staying engaged with their children's schools. Joining Parent Advisory Committees (PACs) can provide opportunities to stay informed about threat assessment protocols and help identify potentially vulnerable areas, such as unmonitored school access points. During my teenage years, I was raised by a single mother of four on welfare, who worked full-time for minimum wage while attending a community college part-time. Because of this, I deeply empathize with parents who may not have the time or resources to participate in PACs. For those who can't, sending a quick email to school principals or administrators to share concerns or suggestions for preventing gun violence is another way to make your voice heard. Joining online safety forums or encouraging children to get involved in student safety groups can also ensure that every perspective is represented.

Finally, fostering strong relationships between students and trusted adults through Community Violence Intervention (CVI) programs is key. Equally important is the responsible storage of firearms.

The Second Amendment protects the right to bear arms, but with that right comes the responsibility to secure firearms safely—especially in homes with children. Securing firearms isn't about limiting ownership; it's about protecting loved ones and preventing accidents. Tragically, over 150 school shootings from 1990 to 2019 were due to accidental discharges, while at least 478 shootings involved firearms that were obtained illegally. Many of these incidents could have been avoided if firearms had been properly secured at home. While this doesn't address the root causes of gun violence, it does help prevent easy access for minors.

Cultivating a culture of kindness, respect, and open communication also goes a long way toward creating safer schools. By taking these steps, communities can work together to make schools safe sanctuaries for learning and growth, free from the dangers of gun violence.

For parents and community members dedicated to preventing gun violence and understanding intervention programs, two outstanding resources offer invaluable insights. The *Creative Interventions Toolkit: A Practical Guide to Stop Interpersonal Violence* provides practical strategies for addressing violence within communities, emphasizing transformative justice and collective action. Meanwhile, the CDC's report, *Community Violence Prevention Resource for Action*, presents evidence-based approaches to reducing violence, equipping families and local leaders with actionable tools to create safer neighborhoods. Both resources are available as free, downloadable PDFs at Creative-Interventions.org, [CDC.gov](CDC.gov), and ASafePlaceBook.com/resources. Together, they empower individuals to take meaningful steps toward violence prevention and community healing.

13

To Ban or Not to Ban AR-15s

Following the Marjory Stoneman Douglas High School mass shooting, parents of the victims and activists from across the country called for a ban on the AR-15 semiautomatic rifle. They argued for the ban, not only because of the rifle's military-grade effectiveness, even in the hands of an amateur, but also because law enforcement failed to confront the shooter while children and teachers were being shot.[1] The plea for banning AR-15s occurred again following the Robb Elementary mass shooting in Uvalde, Texas, because law enforcement waited more than an hour to confront the gunman armed with the same weapon as he fatally shot 19 children and two teachers and injured 17 people.[2] Advocates for the semiautomatic firearm argue that Americans should be afforded the same firearms technology as anyone in the government in order to be able to defend themselves in a potential emergency. Challengers against the AR-15 argue that if a weapon is too intimidating for the police to perform their duty to protect children in an actual emergency, then perhaps it should be banned nationally.

This book does not take a stance on banning the AR-15, adhering to my promise at the outset that proposed solutions would focus exclusively on actions that communities can implement without relying on Congress or the Supreme Court. Nevertheless, I offer one unavoidable, evidence-based observation, backed by statistical facts, regardless of where you stand on the issue of the AR-15 rifle. History demonstrates that banning a single weapon will not restrain determined shooters from committing acts of violence on school grounds, including mass shootings. In fact, between 1990 and 2019, handguns—not AR-15s—were the most frequently used firearms in mass school shootings, accounting for 67.4% of identified weapons. Comparatively, AR-15 and similar XM15 rifles were used in only 4.4% of such incidents. For instance, while AR-15 rifles were involved in tragedies like those at Marjory Stoneman Douglas High School, Rancho Tehama Elementary School, and Santa Monica College, they were not used in other mass school shootings, such as:

Santa Fe High School on May 18, 2018 (10 killed, 13 injured)
<u>Weapons used</u>: Remington 870 shotgun, .38-caliber pistol, improvised explosive devices (IEDs), Molotov Cocktails, pipe bombs and propane tanks.

Marshall County High School on January 23, 2018 (2 killed, 19 injured)
<u>Weapons used</u>: Ruger semi-automatic 9mm pistol, two magazines and Winchester sheath knife.

West Nickel Mines Amish School (Christian elementary and middle school) on October 2, 2016 (6 killed, 5 injured)
<u>Weapons used</u>: Springfield XD 9mm handgun, 1 stun gun, 2 knives, 2 cans of smokeless powder and 600 rounds of ammunition.

El Centro College on July 7, 2016 (6 killed, 9 injured)
<u>Weapons used</u>: AK-74 assault-style rifle.

Umpqua Community College on October 1, 2015 (10 killed, 9 injured)
Weapons used: 2 pistols, 4 rifles, 1 shotgun and 5 magazines.

Sandy Hook Elementary School on December 14, 2012 (28 killed, 2 injured)
Weapons used: .22 caliber Savage Mark II rifle, Bushmaster Model XM15-E2S rifle (similar to an AR-15), two handguns, an Izhmash Saiga-12 12-gauge semi-automatic shotgun and seven 30-round magazines.

Oikos University on April 2, 2012 (7 killed, 3 injured)
Weapons used: .45-caliber semi-automatic handgun.

Northern Illinois University on February 14, 2008 (6 killed, 21 injured)
Weapons used: 12-gauge shotgun, 9mm Glock, 9mm pistol and .38 caliber pistol.

Virginia Tech University on April 16, 2007 (33 killed, 17 injured)
Weapons used: .22-caliber Walther P22 handgun, 9mm Glock 19 handgun, nearly 400 rounds of ammunition, a hunting knife, heavy chains and a hammer.

Red Lake High School on March 21, 2005 (10 killed, 5 injured)
Weapons used: 12-gauge shotgun.

Columbine High School on April 20, 1999 (15 killed, 26 injured)
Weapons used: Intratec TEC-DC9 semi-automatic pistol, Hi-Point 995 Carbine pistol, Savage 67H pump-action shotgun, Stevens 311D double barreled sawed-off shotgun, 100 rounds of ammunition, 99 explosives and 4 knives.

Thurston High School on May 21, 1998 (4 killed, 24 injured)

<u>Weapons used</u>: .22 caliber semiautomatic Ruger rifle, his father's 9mm Glock pistol, .22 caliber Ruger semiautomatic pistol, 1,127 rounds of ammunition and a hunting knife.

Westside Middle School on March 24, 1998 (5 killed, 10 injured)

<u>Weapons used</u>: .60-06 Remington rifle, Ruger .44 Magnum rifle, Universal .30 carbine rifle, Davis industry .38 special two-shot, FIE .380 handgun, Ruger .357 revolver, Remington model 742 .30-06 rifle, Smith & Wesson .38 pistol, Buddie Arms Double Deuce two-shot Derringer, Charter Arms .38 special pistol, Star .380 semiautomatic pistol, six knives, and two speed loader pistols.

University of Iowa on November 1, 1991 (6 killed, 1 injured)

<u>Weapons used</u>: Taurus .38-caliber revolver, .22-caliber handgun.

*For more details about each shooting, please see my other books, *The Ultimate U.S. School Shooting Reference Guide, Volumes 1-3*.

14

Alyssa's Law

February 14, 2018, was a day of profound loss and a catalyst for activism at my alma mater in Parkland, Florida. As documented in *The Ultimate U.S. School Shooting Reference Guide, Volumes 1-3*, this sorrow has echoed through countless American communities for decades. One of the precious lives lost that day at Marjory Stoneman Douglas High School was Alyssa Alhadeff, a 14-year-old freshman. Alyssa was not just a bright scholar and talented soccer player; she was a daughter, a friend, and a vibrant young soul with dreams and aspirations. Tragically, Alyssa was shot eight times in her English classroom. It is heartbreaking to think that, had fact-based, common-sense school safety measures been in place, Alyssa and some of the other 17 victims might have survived the tragedy.

Alyssa's Law requires every public school classroom to be equipped with panic alarms directly linked to local law enforcement, providing a critical lifeline in moments of crisis.[1] This law transcends political lines and is of vital interest to teachers and students in every school across the United States. While *Alyssa's Law* may not prevent the next school shooting, it can help mitigate the loss of life during an active threat. The precious seconds that panic buttons can save during an active school shooting response can literally make the difference between life and death. Originally introduced in 2014 following the

Newtown, Connecticut shooting, the law was later renamed *Alyssa's Law* to honor Alyssa Alhadeff. This legislation was passed in New Jersey (Alyssa's home state) in 2019, in Florida in 2020, in Texas and Tennessee in 2023, and in Utah in 2024. Perhaps your state could be next to help save lives by passing this law.

When I first moved to Virginia for a librarian job in 2022, Lori Alhadeff, the founder of the nonprofit organization Make Our Schools Safe, encouraged me to contact my governor to request the passage of *Alyssa's Law* (HB 1046). After I wrote to Virginia Governor Glenn Youngkin on June 2, 2022, I received a response indicating that the Superintendent of Public Instruction, Jillian Balow, was reaching out to Virginia school division superintendents for their views on additional school safety measures the state should take in the wake of the mass shooting tragedy at Robb Elementary School in Uvalde, Texas on May 24, 2022. After Lori Alhadeff testified in front of the Virginia House committee in 2024, lawmakers voted to table the bill, meaning no further action would be taken on it due to funding concerns, not citing objections to the bill itself.[2]

While I may not be skilled at persuading legislators to support common-sense laws that could save lives, I am continually impressed by Lori Alhadeff's tenacity and ability to inspire lawmakers across the country to not only consider, but also pass such vital legislation through the grassroots efforts of her nonprofit organization, Make Our Schools Safe. As a result, I asked Lori directly:

Q: What are you doing differently so that other parents can effectively advocate for the adoption of *Alyssa's Law* in their own states?

Lori: Advocating for *Alyssa's Law* requires a combination of strategic planning, persistence, and collaboration. Here's what I've found effective:

- **Building Relationships with Lawmakers**: Establishing direct and consistent communication with legislators, their staff, and other stakeholders to educate them about the law's purpose and urgency.

- **Partnering with Advocacy Groups**: Collaborating with organizations like Make Our Schools Safe (MOSS) and other safety-focused groups amplifies the message and provides additional credibility. (Teachers Unions, 911 Centers, Law Enforcement....)

- **Presenting Data and Stories**: Providing lawmakers with compelling statistics on school violence and real-life stories of lives lost due to delayed emergency response times helps them connect emotionally to the issue. I will go to Committee Hearings and give a testimonial.

- **Mobilizing Grassroots Efforts**: Encouraging parents, students, and community members to contact their representatives and attend public hearings or events shows lawmakers the widespread support for *Alyssa's Law*. Our MOSS Clubs have lobbied in Colorado to try to get *Alyssa's Law* passed.

- **Utilizing Media and Public Platforms**: Raising awareness through media campaigns and public events draws attention to the cause and puts pressure on legislators to act via Facebook, Instagram, and X.

- **We Have an Interactive Clickable Map on Our Website**: Video Testimonials and Emails to legislators of the importance of passing *Alyssa's Law* in their home state.

I also emphasize the importance of persistence—sometimes it takes multiple attempts and re-engaging lawmakers to make progress.

Q: In your experience, what kind of feedback are you getting from lawmakers? Why is *Alyssa's Law* getting bipartisan support?

Lori: Lawmakers appreciate that *Alyssa's Law* is non-partisan and rooted in the universal goal of protecting children in schools. Here's why it garners bipartisan support:

- **Focus on Safety Over Politics**: *Alyssa's Law* doesn't push a political agenda; it addresses a clear need for enhanced communication and response systems during emergencies.

- **Data-Driven Solutions**: The law provides a concrete, measurable solution—silent panic alarm systems—that enhances existing school safety measures without adding significant controversy or financial burden.

- **Universal Agreement on Protecting Children**: Regardless of political affiliation, lawmakers recognize the shared responsibility to ensure students and staff are safe in educational environments.

- *Alyssa's Law* has passed unanimously in all 7 states.

Q: Do you have any stories of the positive impact *Alyssa's Law* has had so far? Has there been any case in which a school shooting or other violence was prevented?

Lori: *Alyssa's Law* has already made significant strides by improving communication and response times in schools where it has been implemented. While it's challenging to quantify specific instances where violence was entirely prevented, there are documented cases where the presence of panic alarms has:

- **Reduced Response Time**: Schools equipped with these systems have reported faster coordination with law enforcement during emergencies, which could be critical in de-escalating threats. For example, the wearable panic button had shown effectiveness in the Apalachee School Shooting.

- **Enhanced Peace of Mind**: Both students and staff feel safer knowing there's an additional layer of protection in place, fostering a healthier learning environment.

In just six and a half minutes, a former student entered the campus of Marjory Stoneman Douglas High School and opened fire with an AR-15 semiautomatic rifle, killing 17 children and teachers and injuring 17 more. In an active shooter situation, every second matters. The moment a threat is identified, anyone with a panic button or mobile app-based system could save lives by instantly alerting law enforcement to the shooter's location—giving students precious time to escape or shelter in place. This tool is designed to strengthen, not replace, existing school safety measures. *Alyssa's Law* offers a practical, noncontroversial, and cost-effective solution that could help prevent tragedies like Parkland, Sandy Hook, Red Lake, Rancho Tehama, Virginia Tech, and Columbine. To learn more about *Alyssa's Law*, the Make Our Schools Safe nonprofit, and the Make Our Schools Safe (MOSS) Club—committed to fostering a culture of school safety—visit MakeOurSchoolsSafe.org.

15

Stand for the Silent

When I had the humbling privilege of speaking with Kirk Smalley, I couldn't have anticipated the emotional impact of hearing his personal story of loss. Kirk's 11-year-old son, Ty, tragically died by suicide after enduring two years of relentless bullying at school. Since that heartbreaking day, Kirk and his wife, Laura, have dedicated their lives to raising awareness about bullying and its devastating consequences. They've reached millions of children, sparking important conversations and inspiring change.

After losing my sister to firearm suicide in 2022, I've wrestled with a profound weight of grief and the haunting question: could I have done more to prevent her death? In my research on school shootings, I discovered that out of 1,204 incidents, 214 (17.7%) ended in suicide. Of these, 120 shooters took only their own lives. Disturbingly, these suicides—when no other victims are involved—are often omitted from government school shooting reports. This oversight creates an incomplete understanding of the broader problem of gun violence in schools. Yet, the impact of suicide is far-reaching, rippling through communities and leaving loved ones grappling with unimaginable pain. I hope and pray you never face such a preventable and tragic loss.

Stand for the Silent (SFTS) is a nonprofit organization that tackles school bullying and teen suicide with a powerful mix of factual evidence, emotional testimonials, and community engagement. I strongly encourage you to research their work and consider starting a Stand for the Silent chapter at your child's school.

Recently, I asked Kirk, "Why do you feel it is so important for parents to address the issue of bullying and teen suicide?" He responded, "I feel it's so very important for caregivers to address the subjects of bullying and suicide because I have spoken to thousands upon thousands of our young people that feel like, 'No one gets it. No one cares. I'm all alone in this. No one has ever gone through this or felt this way.' We HAVE to let them know they are NOT alone, and we DO care."

Testimonials for Stand for the Silent:

Below is a collection of some of the powerful testimonies of how Stand for the Silent has positively impacted the lives of teachers and children following Kirk's presentation in their schools. The first testimony is from a teacher in Chicago who invited Kirk to speak at their school:

"Your presentation was amazing. We are still talking about it and we will remember it, hopefully forever. You are a great presenter and clearly a genuine person. Maybe you could return in a few years??? By the way, three students spoke with our social worker yesterday in the afternoon about having suicidal thoughts."

"Kirk,

Your speech was powerful and I don't know if you get this but if you do thank you because if I was being honest if I didn't hear your voice I think I would have taken my life. My voice can be heard and I wish I could travel with your help."

"I'm not sure if you are the same person that spoke to my school in I believe early 2011. But if you are I just want to say thank you. On

November 29, 2010, my best friend committed suicide, not long after someone from Stand for the Silent came to our school and spoke to us. If you're the same person you stood in the hall with me for about 20 minutes just talking with me as I was struggling to even want to be on this earth after losing my best friend. You played a part in saving my life and I could never thank you enough. I still have the Stand for the Silent card you gave me that day in a wallet that I keep put up and a bracelet that finally broke last year. But again, I just want to thank you for just speaking to me and being present in a dark time in my life and giving me words of encouragement that kept me on this earth and has allowed me to become an amazing person and a mother. So once again, thank you so much. I still do and will always and forever stand for the silent. God bless."

10 Strategies for Bullying Prevention for Schools

Preventing bullying in schools requires a continuous effort from parents, educators, administrators, and students, but achieving real change is within reach. Stand for the Silent teaches that in order for true change to take place, the culture of a school must be transformed. But it's not as difficult as it sounds. By implementing a year-round bullying prevention program, setting clear expectations for faculty and staff, and establishing guidelines for addressing incidents, students and educators can create a nurturing environment. This way, both students and adults can foster a culture of empathy and respect.

The following 10 strategies for bullying prevention were borrowed directly from the Stand for the Silent website, with permission from Mr. Kirk Smalley:

1. Establish school-wide policies and classroom procedures pertaining to bullying that are distributed to students, parents, and teachers.

2. Depict on bulletin boards and in hallways that school and classrooms are bully-free zones, and that students treat each other with respect.

3. Develop strategies to recognize and reward positive social behavior.

4. Speak with ALL involved in a bullying situation separately and in private.

5. Develop separate intervention plans for children who are bullied, children who participate as bystanders, and children who bully others. Some intervention plans may need to include steps to address circumstances where a student who has been bullied also bullies others or vice versa.

6. Be mindful of class seating arrangements to promote positive role models and limit access.

7. Hold periodic class meetings and assemblies to remind children of bullying prevention.

8. Contact parents of all students involved in a bullying incident; meet separately with parents of each student to provide information about bullying; explain school's bullying protocol; and address the specifics of the situation. Do not identify names of other students. Provide support and clarifications to address parents' emotional reactions, as well as solicit parent input and review intervention plan. Assess extent of social/emotional/family problems in conjunction with the school counselor, and ensure that appropriate referrals are given to parents.

9. Establish procedures for documenting episodes of bullying and intervention.

10. Assign all students classroom allies/buddies and periodically rearrange the assignments.

In the aftermath of tragedy, unexpected heroes often arise from the ashes. The true power lies in the ability to simply listen, understand, and empathize with others' pain, fostering connections that can lead to meaningful change. The volunteers at Stand for the Silent embody this spirit. They are dedicated to showing those affected by bullying and suicidal thoughts that they are not alone and that they are cared for. In the united community effort to create safe learning environments, every school can benefit from a tested and effective, year-round bullying prevention program. To learn more and find out how to start a Stand for the Silent chapter at your child's school, visit StandForTheSilent.org.

16

Apps That Can Help Save Children's Lives

There are two types of mobile apps that could help save a child's life before and during a school shooting: one that allows parents to monitor their child's mobile phone activities, and another that functions as a panic button in the event of an active shooter threat. For the sake of transparency, I receive no financial incentives for recommending any of the following mobile apps. In the chapter "How to Prevent the Next School Shooting," I emphasized the importance of actively monitoring your children's journals, phones, class assignments, and online activity. Numerous examples show that shooters often reveal warning signs before engaging in a school shooting or contemplating suicide. Mobile apps like OurPact can teach kids healthy technology and screen time habits while giving parents insights into how their child uses their device. This app is recommended by Clayton Cranford, also known as the "Cyber Safety Cop." Clayton is the CEO of Total Safety Solutions, an organization specializing in internet safety tips, drug use prevention assemblies for K-12 students in both public and private schools, and violence prevention through behavioral threat assessment training. He is a former school resource officer and the author of *Parenting in the Digital World*, which is currently in its 3rd edition and now available in Spanish.

I had the privilege of interviewing Clayton on my podcast in 2024. What surprised me the most was that kindergarten through third-grade schools are inviting Clayton to talk to their students about the dangers of using smartphones and social media. He revealed a disturbing fact: social media and prolonged smartphone use contribute to negative mental health and even suicide among young teens. To encourage internet safety for teens, he advises parents to wait until their children are 16 before buying them a smartphone. If a younger child needs a phone, Clayton suggests buying them a flip phone. It is understandable that young people may feel they would be missing out on a social life without a smartphone. If your children already have smartphones and tablets, using an app like OurPact can help monitor their online safety. For more information, go to the following OurPact URL for a subscription discount: https://app.ourpact.com/signup/cybersafetycop .

The second type of mobile app that could help save a child's life during an active shooter threat is an app that immediately alerts law enforcement of the location of the threat, thereby reducing response time in an emergency. Such tools enhance existing school safety measures and empower school personnel to protect their students and maintain a secure environment. Mobile panic button apps like SchoolGuard® and SaferWatch meet the requirements of *Alyssa's Law*.[1][2] Both apps notify 911/Emergency Services instantly and provide local law enforcement with a mapped location of the threat when the panic button is activated.[3][4] Each mobile app also offers unique additional safety features, such as the ability to submit videos, photos, and audio to help law enforcement assess the threat, and the capability to send instant alerts to all approved users on the property. For more information on each of these school safety apps, go to:

- SchoolGuard®: https://guard911.com/services/schoolguard/
- SaferWatch: https://www.saferwatchapp.com/

The integration of mobile apps for monitoring and emergency response can play a crucial role in enhancing the safety and well-being of children in today's digital age. By leveraging apps like OurPact, parents can cultivate healthier tech habits and ensure they are alerted to potential warning signs exhibited by their children. Simultaneously, panic button apps such as SchoolGuard® and SaferWatch provide an essential layer of protection during critical moments, complying with *Alyssa's Law* to expedite emergency responses. These non-partisan tools, combined with informed and proactive parenting, can create a safer environment and empower communities to take decisive steps toward preventing and responding to school shootings. Let's continue to advocate for and implement these life-saving technologies to safeguard the futures of all children.

17

A Positive Note

To end this lesson on a positive note, I humbly present the following scene:

Imagine a warm, summer afternoon outside your window in the middle of your work day. The sun streams through your office window, casting a golden glow on the framed picture of your child and their two closest friends, dressed in their high school graduation gowns. The rhythmic clicks on nearby computer keyboards and the distant hum of office chatter create a backdrop of normalcy. Your child graduated with high marks and has been working hard all summer to save money for their first car. You have told your colleagues you couldn't be more proud. Your cell phone ring breaks your concentration and your child's smiling face appears in the caller I.D. Your first thought is, "They never call while I am at work. There must be something wrong." A wave of anxiety washes over you as you debate whether to answer right away or let it go to voicemail. Your heart races, and you take a deep breath before quickly stepping outside the office to answer your phone.

Parent: Hello?
Child: Hey, it's me. I have to tell you something...

Parent: What happened? What's wrong?
Child: I just opened the mail and...I'm going!
Parent: You're going?
Child: I got in to my first college choice!

You both yell with excitement and do a little happy dance, your heart swelling with pride. A colleague passes by and glances at you with a curious expression on their face. You compose yourself, but just barely.

Parent: That's so great, sweetheart! I'm so proud of you!
Child: I can't thank you enough. I know that I have been difficult these past few years, but I know that you have sacrificed so much for me. I know it wasn't easy, but I would have never made it without you guiding and protecting me.

Tears well up in your eyes as you hold back from swallowing a frog in your throat. You compose yourself as you take a slow, deep breath to prevent any tears from escaping your eyes.

Child: ...Are you still there?
Parent: Yup. That's my job. You're my child and I love you. But what about...?
Child: Don't worry. Just to be safe, I will live off-campus with a friend. And I have a part-time job lined up.

You want to offer your child a flood of advice and a list of safety precautions, but instead, you simply say...

Parent: You're so smart and grown up.

You grip the phone tightly, your knuckles turning white. A tear finally escapes and you quickly wipe it away, hoping no one notices.

Child: I just want you to know that I got it from here.
I feel confident and strong because that is what
you have been for me. I can't wait to see what the
future holds!
Parent: Me too, sweetheart. Me too.
Child: Love you!
Parent: Love you more.

End.

I hope this book and *The Ultimate U.S. School Shooting Reference Guide Volumes 1-3*, serve as valuable resources—ones that provide insightful, informative, and empowering content for generations to come. This immense undertaking has been a labor of love, requiring seven years of meticulous research, interpretation, writing, illustration, and editing—all completed without any outside funding. During this process, I worked full-time, pursued a master's degree part-time, earned my black belt in Olympic-style Taekwondo for the second time, and made time for my family—though not much for sleep. My goal has always been to simplify this information and make it accessible to you, in the hope that it will save lives, spark constructive dialogue, and inspire communities to take preventive action based on factual, nonpartisan data.

Some may call me naïve or overly optimistic—arguing that "no one truly cares" about saving children's lives despite public declarations—but I refuse to lose hope. As long as there are dedicated individuals willing to fight until safety, peace, and empathy become pillars of our national culture, hope will endure. Gun violence must never become an accepted norm in our lives.

I pray that you, your children, and your grandchildren live safe, happy, and fulfilling lives—a privilege tragically denied to far too many victims of gun violence. Keep fighting by actively participating in Community Violence Intervention (CVI) programs and Parent Advisory Committees (PACs). Stay mentally strong by learning and applying emotional intelligence and mastery. Remain vigilant to potential warning signs at home and in school settings. Practice consistent, safe, and secure storage of firearms in gun safes. Every child deserves to grow up in peace. You are not alone. Together, we will overcome this challenge and build a safer tomorrow.

With much love and respect, thank you for reading and sharing my research with your community.

Sincerely,
~ Luis the Librarian

About the Author

Luis D. Aponte.
Photo by Bob Lasky.

Luis D. Aponte is a librarian, U.S. Air Force veteran, and the author of four books and eBooks on school shootings: *A Safe Place: How to Prevent the Next School Shooting* and *The Ultimate U.S. School Shooting Reference Guide, Volumes 1-3*. His work has been published in Virginia's Mt. Vernon Gazette and Fairfax Connection newspapers and the peer-reviewed EDUCATION journal. Luis resides in Virginia, where he enjoys "forest bathing" in national parks with his wife, making films, and spoiling their adopted orange tabby cat, Ellie.

In 1992-1993, Luis attended Marjory Stoneman Douglas High School in Parkland, Florida, but dropped out during his junior year due to the threat of gun violence on campus. Approximately 25 years later, the same school experienced one of the worst school shootings in U.S. history. Since then, Luis has dedicated his research skills as a librarian to finding patterns in 1,204 U.S. school shooting incidents over 30 years, aiming to help save children's lives.

Originally from Savannah, Georgia, Luis earned his master's degree in Library and Information Science from the University of South Florida, his bachelor's degree in Communications – Film & Video from Florida Atlantic University, and his associate's degree in Computer Science from Broward College in Florida, all with honors. He was also a member and the historian for his local chapters of the Golden Key International Honour Society and Phi Theta Kappa International College Honor Society.

Luis hopes his books on school shootings will help bring communities together to save lives. Children and educators deserve to feel safe in schools without the threat of gun violence.

Connect With Me

Website: www.ASafePlaceBook.com
Linktree: https://linktr.ee/LuisAponte

Facebook: @ASafePlaceBook
Instagram: @ASafePlaceBook
Bluesky: @ASafePlaceBook.bsky.social
YouTube: @ASafePlaceBook

Other Titles by Luis D. Aponte

eBooks available on **Draft2Digital.com**.
Physical books available on **IngramSpark.com**.
A Safe Place is also available as an eAudiobook on major platforms via **Voices by INaudio**.

A Safe Place: How to Prevent the Next School Shooting

The Ultimate U.S. School Shooting Reference Guide: Volume 1: 1990-1999

The Ultimate U.S. School Shooting Reference Guide:
Volume 2: 2000-2009

The Ultimate U.S. School Shooting Reference Guide:
Volume 3: 2010-2019

Book Discussion Guide

Thank you so much for dedicating your valuable time to read my book. Your willingness to engage with my work means the world to me. I hope you found it thought-provoking, insightful and helpful. I encourage you to use the following questions to spark meaningful discussions with friends, family, book clubs and in school classrooms.

1. What assumptions did you have about this book before reading it? Did your opinions change after you finished it?

2. Do you know anyone who has been affected by gun violence? If so, what happened, and how did it impact both them and you?

3. Before reading this book, how familiar were you with patterns related to school shootings?

4. Have you or someone you know ever experienced bullying? How did you or they handle the situation? What do you think you or they could have done better in this situation?

5. Do you think that having panic button mobile apps can help save lives in schools? Why or why not?

6. Which of the author's research findings surprised you the most? Why?

7. Which of the proposed solutions for preventing the next school shooting seem the most achievable to you? Why?

8. If you are a parent, how do you teach your child(ren) to develop emotional intelligence and mastery?

9. After reading this book, what are your thoughts on parents using mobile apps to monitor their child's activities on their devices?

10. Were there any solutions in the book that you disagreed with? Why or why not?

11. Are there any community-based solutions the author did not mention that you believe would help prevent the next school shooting?

12. How did you feel about the author's position on AR-15 semiautomatic rifles?

13. Do you think the suggested solutions would appeal to parents regardless of their political views? Why or why not?

14. Did you find the information in the book to be credible and nonpartisan? Please explain.

15. Who do you think would benefit the most from reading this book?

I hope the insights featured in this book positively impacts your family and community for generations. Please share your honest opinions about this book on the website where you purchased it. Thank you!

Notes

Chapter 1: The Four Deaths

1. Hofheinz, D. (2024, April 6). Majority of billionaires in Palm Beach got richer ... but some, including Trump, did not. *The Palm Beach Post*. Retrieved from https://www.palmbeachpost.com/story/news/2024/04/06/worlds-richest-palm-beach-is-home-to-at-least-58-forbes-billionaires/73218737007/
2. Andone, D., Jackson, A., & Gomez, I. (2018, March 24). The March for Our Lives isn't just happening in the United States. *CNN*. Retrieved from https://www.cnn.com/2018/03/24/world/march-for-our-lives-around-the-world-trnd/index.html
3. Adashi E.Y.; Cohen, I.G. (2015, November 5). Selective Regrets: The "Dickey Amendments" 20 Years Later. *JAMA Health Forum*. Retrieved from https://jamanetwork.com/channels/health-forum/fullarticle/2760581
4. Pollack, A., & Eden, M. (2019). *Why Meadow died: The people and policies that created the Parkland shooter and endanger America's students* (pp. 155-169). Post Hill Press.
5. Travis, S., Huriash, L.J., & Olmeda, R. (2021, April 21). Broward Schools Superintendent Robert Runcie charged with perjury; his lawyer says he doesn't know why. *Sun Sentinel and Yahoo! Sports*. Retrieved from https://sports.yahoo.com/broward-schools-superintendent-robert-runcie-021300866.html
6. (Travis, S., Huriash, L.J., & Olmeda, 2021)
7. Travis, S. (2018, April 24). Broward schools ready to combat what they call fake news. South Florida. *South Florida Sun Sentinel*. Retrieved from https://www.sun-sentinel.com/news/education/fl-florida-school-shooting-fake-news-20180424-story.html
8. Moore, M. H., Petrie, C. V., Braga, A. A., & McLaughlin, B. L. (2003). *Deadly lessons: understanding lethal school violence* (p. 186). Washington, D.C.: The National Academy Press.
9. Education Week Staff. (2018, August 24). Should Teachers Carry Guns? The Debate, Explained. *Education Week*. Retrieved March 19, 2022 from https://www.edweek.org/leadership/should-teachers-carry-guns-the-debate-explained/2018/08
10. Duke, C. (2018, September 14). Various schools across Green Country do not use metal detectors; believe it sets wrong tone. *2 News Oklahoma*. Retrieved

March 19, 2022 from https://www.kjrh.com/news/local-news/various-schools-across-green-country-do-not-use-metal-detectors-believe-it-sets-wrong-tone

11. Foster, A. (2018, November 13). Community considers metal detectors after guns found at schools. *3 WBTV On Your Side*. Retrieved March 19, 2022 from https://www.wbtv.com/2018/11/14/community-considers-metal-detectors-after-guns-found-schools/

12. Davis, J. (2019, January 25). Indiana district adds metal detectors to campuses. *Campus Security & Life Safety*. Retrieved March 19, 2022 from https://campuslifesecurity.com/articles/2019/01/25/indiana-district-adds-metal-detectors-to-campuses.aspx?admgarea=Topics

13. Mason, J., & Trotta, D. (2018, May 4). Trump back in step with NRA after doubts over Parkland shooting. *Reuters*. Retrieved from https://www.reuters.com/article/us-usa-guns-trump/trump-back-in-step-with-nra-after-doubts-over-parkland-shooting-idUSKBN1I50ZR

Chapter 3: Bookmarks in Life

1. A look back at the Aurora, Colorado, movie theater shooting 5 years later. (2017, July 20). *ABC News*. Retrieved from https://abcnews.go.com/US/back-aurora-colorado-movie-theater-shooting-years/story?id=48730066

2. Jiang, J. (2018, September 14). How Teens and Parents Navigate Screen Time and Device Distractions. *Pew Research Center*. Retrieved from http://www.pewinternet.org/2018/08/22/how-teens-and-parents-navigate-screen-time-and-device-distractions/

3. Hogg, D. and Hogg, L. (2018, June 19). *#NeverAgain*, New York (p. 88). Random House.

4. Rosenberg, E. (2018, March 27). A new epithet emerges for Parkland teens calling for more gun control: Nazis. *The Washington Post*. Retrieved from https://www.washingtonpost.com/news/politics/wp/2018/03/27/a-new-epithet-emerges-for-parkland-teens-calling-for-more-gun-control-nazis/

5. (Hogg & Hogg, 2018, p. 45)

6. Pollack, A., & Eden, M. (2019). *Why Meadow died: The people and policies that created the Parkland shooter and endanger America's students* (p. 43). Post Hill Press.

7. O'Matz, M., & Travis, S. (2018, May 12). Schools' culture of tolerance lets students like Nikolas Cruz slide. *South Florida Sun Sentinel*. Retrieved from https://www.sun-sentinel.com/local/broward/parkland/florida-school-shooting/fl-florida-school-shooting-discipline-20180510-story.html

8. Hogg, D. and Hogg, L. (2018, June 19). *#NeverAgain*, New York (p. 19). Random House.

Chapter 5: Everyone in the Community Has a Role

1. Leung, R. (2018, April 12). The mind of a school shooter. *CBS News*. Retrieved from https://www.cbsnews.com/news/the-mind-of-a-school-shooter/

Chapter 6: Understanding School Gun Violence

1. U.S. Department of Justice & Federal Bureau of Investigation. (2019, April). *Active Shooter Incidents in the United States from 2000-2018* [PDF file]. Retrieved from https://www.fbi.gov/file-repository/active-shooter-incidents-2000-2018.pdf/view
2. Federal Bureau of Investigation. (n.d.). *Active shooter resources*. Retrieved March 19, 2022 from https://www.fbi.gov/about/partnerships/office-of-partner-engagement/active-shooter-resources
3. U.S. Department of Justice & Federal Bureau of Investigation. (2019, April). *Active Shooter Incidents in the United States from 2000-2018* [PDF file]. Retrieved from https://www.fbi.gov/file-repository/active-shooter-incidents-2000-2018.pdf/view
4. United States Secret Service & United States Department of Education. (2004, July). *The final report and findings of the safe school initiative: implications for the prevention of school attacks in the United States* [PDF file] (p. 9). Retrieved from https://www2.ed.gov/admins/lead/safety/preventingattacksreport.pdf
5. (United States Secret Service & United States Department of Education, 2004, p. 8)
6. United States Government Accountability Office. (2020, June). *Report to congressional requesters: K-12 education characteristics of school shootings* [PDF file]. Retrieved March 19, 2022 from https://www.gao.gov/assets/gao-20-455.pdf
7. (United States Government Accountability Office, 2020, p. 8)

Chapter 8: Roots and Myths Behind Motivations

1. Gunman could serve up to 40 years in prison after guilty plea. (2007, October 26). *ESPN*. Retrieved from https://www.espn.com/mens-college-basketball/news/story?id=3080781
2. E. Ky. man sentenced to 3 life terms in slayings. (2014, June 6). *WLKY Louisville*. Retrieved from https://www.wlky.com/article/e-ky-man-sentenced-to-3-life-terms-in-slayings/3750296

3. Ward, K., & Estep, B. (2013, January 15). Man charged in shooting that kills 2, injures 1 at Hazard Community and Technical College. *Lexington Herald Leader.* Retrieved from https://www.kentucky.com/news/local/crime/article44397618.html
4. Puente, K. (2024, March 24). Timeline: The Covenant School shooting and the dramatic year that followed. *The Tennessean.* Retrieved from https://www.tennessean.com/story/news/local/2024/03/24/covenant-school-shooting-timeline-recovery-covenant-church-covenant-school/73016795007/
5. Roberson, A. (2023, November 27). Victims of Covenant School shooting include daughter of pastor, head of school. *The Tennessean.* Retrieved from https://www.tennessean.com/story/news/local/2023/03/27/who-are-the-nashville-school-shooting-victims-covenant-presbyterian/70053940007/
6. Radford, A., Hammond, E., Sangal, A., Powell, T.B., & Watson, M. (2024, December 17). December 17, 2024, Madison, Wisconsin, school shooting news. *CNN.* Retrieved from https://edition.cnn.com/us/live-news/madison-wisconsin-school-shooting-12-17-24/index.html
7. Tsui, K., Yeung, J., Jackson, A., & Watson, M. (2024, December 18). Unanswered questions remain about teen who allegedly opened fire on Wisconsin school as details emerge about her home life. *CNN.* Retrieved from https://www.cnn.com/2024/12/18/us/madison-school-shooting-wednesday/index.html
8. Wallman, B., McMahon, P., O'Matz, M., & Bryan, S. (2018, Feb 25). Accused shooter lost, lonely Nikolas Cruz had a troubled life long before attack. *Orlando Sentinel* (p. A1). Retrieved from https://www.proquest.com/newspapers/accused-shooter-lost-lonely-nikolas-cruz-had/docview/2642333281/se-2
9. Rogers, B. (2011, May 17). Gun owner charged in shootings at Ross Elementary. *Chron.* Retrieved from https://www.chron.com/news/houston-texas/article/Gun-owner-charged-in-shootings-at-Ross-Elementary-1692198.php
10. 3 hurt when gun discharges at school. (2011, April 19). *KPRC 2 Houston.* Retrieved from https://www.click2houston.com/news/2011/04/19/3-hurt-when-gun-discharges-at-school/
11. Virginia Tech shootings fast facts. (2024, May 2). *CNN.* Retrieved from https://www.cnn.com/2013/10/31/us/virginia-tech-shootings-fast-facts/
12. Landman, P. (2013) Psychiatric medications and school shooters [PDF file]. *School Shooters.Info* (p. 1-6). Retrieved from https://schoolshooters.info/sites/default/files/Psychiatric%20Medications.pdf

Chapter 9: Overlooked Warning Signs

1. Kifner, J., Bragg, R., Johnson, D., & Verhovek, S. H. (1998, March 29). From wild talk and friendship to five deaths in a schoolyard. *New York Times, The*. Retrieved from https://www.nytimes.com/1998/03/29/us/from-wild-talk-and-friendship-to-five-deaths-in-a-schoolyard.html?sec=&spon=&pagewanted=all
2. Langman Ph.D., P. (2014). Charles Andrew Williams: sorting out the contradictions [PDF file]. *SchoolShooters.info* (pp. 7-8). Retrieved from https://schoolshooters.info/sites/default/files/williams_contradictions_1.1.pdf
3. Jefferson County Sheriff's Office. (2017, June 25). Columbine documents [PDF file]. *Internet Archive*, pp. JC-001-026013 - JC-001-026015. Retrieved from https://archive.org/details/columbine_201706/mode/2up?view=theater
4. (Langman Ph.D., 2014, p. 7)
5. (Jefferson County Sheriff's Office, 2017, p. JC-001-026013)
6. Virginia Tech Review Panel. (2007, April 16). *Mass shootings at Virginia Tech: report of the review panel presented to governor Kaine Commonwealth of Virginia* [PDF file] (pp. 21 & 25). Retrieved from https://scholar.lib.vt.edu/prevail/docs/VTReviewPanelReport.pdf
7. (Virginia Tech Review Panel, 2007, p. 50)
8. Pegues, J. (2018, February 15). Florida school shooting: FBI got call about suspect a year before shooting. *CBS News*. Retrieved from https://www.cbsnews.com/news/fbi-youtube-video-investigation-florida-shooting-suspect-nikolas-cruz-details-today/
9. Andone, D. (2018, February 26). The warning signs almost everyone missed. *CNN*. Retrieved from https://www.cnn.com/2018/02/25/us/nikolas-cruz-warning-signs/index.html

Chapter 11: Mass vs. Conventional School Shootings

1. Investigative Assistance for Violent Crimes Act of 2012, Pub. L. No. 112-265 (2013) [PDF file]. Retrieved from https://www.congress.gov/112/plaws/publ265/PLAW-112publ265.pdf
2. U.S. Department of Justice Office of Justice Programs. (2013). *Analysis of recent mass shootings*. Retrieved from https://www.ojp.gov/ncjrs/virtual-library/abstracts/analysis-recent-mass-shootings
3. Nichols, C. (2017, October 4). How is a 'mass shooting' defined? *PolitiFact*. Retrieved from https://www.politifact.com/article/2017/oct/04/mass-shooting-what-does-it-mean/

4. Everytown for Gun Safety Support Fund. (2016). *Analysis of school shootings* [PDF file] (p. 1). Retrieved from https://everytownresearch.org/documents/2015/04/analysis-of-school-shootings.pdf
5. Community Violence Intervention Leaders Unveil Historic Action Plan to Sustain and Scale the Field. (2024, August 16). *The Health Alliance for Violence Intervention*. Retrieved from https://www.thehavi.org/community-violence-intervention-leaders-unveil-historic-action-plan-to-sustain-and-scale-the-field#:~:text=%E2%80%9CThrough%20CVI%20strategies%2C%20we%20should,David%20M
6. About Virginia Satir. (n.d.). *The University of North Carolina of Chapel Hill*. Retrieved from https://satir.web.unc.edu/about-virginia-satir/

Chapter 12: How to Prevent the Next School Shooting

1. Landry, L. (2019, April 3). Why emotional intelligence is important in leadership. *Harvard Business School Online*. Retrieved from https://online.hbs.edu/blog/post/emotional-intelligence-in-leadership
2. Murphy-Shigematsu Ed.D., S. (2016, March 11). The Japanese Art of Acceptance: Shikata ga nai. *Psychology Today*. Retrieved from https://www.psychologytoday.com/us/blog/finding-meaning-in-lifes-struggles/201603/the-japanese-art-of-acceptance-shikata-ga-nai?msockid=310f3f36862b69aa28762e8c879c6825
3. Teen-ager charged in fatal shootings. (1995, September 27). *Springfield News-Leader, The*, p. 13A. Retrieved from https://www.newspapers.com/image/207677156/?terms=Ryan%2BSpornitz
4. Bad blood between schools. (1995, September 27). *Daily Tribune, The* (p. 12B). Retrieved from https://www.newspapers.com/image/244773135/?terms=Jerrell%2BFrazier%2C
5. National School Safety Center. (2010, March 3). *School Associated Violent Deaths* [PDF file] (p. 12). Retrieved from https://files.eric.ed.gov/fulltext/ED519244.pdf
6. Bad blood between schools. (1995, September 27). *Daily Tribune, The* (p. 12B). Retrieved from https://www.newspapers.com/image/244773135/?terms=Jerrell%2BFrazier%2C
7. Knoll, James & Annas, George. (2016). *Mass Shootings and Mental Illness* [PDF file]. 10.1176/appi.books.9781615378562.lg04.
8. This day in history: February 14, 2018: Teen gunman kills 17, injures 17 at Parkland, Florida high school. (2024). *History*. Retrieved from https://www.history.com/this-day-in-history/parkland-marjory-stoneman-douglas-school-shooting
9. National Center for Education Statistics. (2019, August). *Table 233.70: Percentage of public schools with security staff present at least once a week, and percent-

age with security staff routinely carrying a firearm, by selected school characteristics: 2005–06 through 2017-18. Retrieved from https://nces.ed.gov/programs/digest/d19/tables/dt19_233.70.asp
10. Knoll, James & Annas, George. (2016). *Mass Shootings and Mental Illness* [PDF file]. 10.1176/appi.books.9781615378562.lg04.
11. MentalHealth.gov. (2017, August 29). *Mental health myths and facts.* Retrieved from https://www.mentalhealth.gov/basics/mental-health-myths-facts
12. Corthell, K. (2014, September 9). The role of mental health counselors in public schools. *Georgia State University* [PDF file] (p. 21). Retrieved from https://core.ac.uk/download/pdf/129452857.pdf
13. Safety assessment and intervention. (n.d.). *Sandy Hook Promise.* Retrieved from https://www.sandyhookpromise.org/our-programs/program-overview/program-partners/
14. United States Secret Service & United States Department of Education. (2004, July). *The final report and findings of the safe school initiative: implications for the prevention of school attacks in the United States* [PDF file]. Retrieved from https://www2.ed.gov/admins/lead/safety/preventingattacksreport.pdf
15. Leung, R. (2018, April 12). The mind of a school shooter. *CBS News.* Retrieved from https://www.cbsnews.com/news/the-mind-of-a-school-shooter/
16. Scholdkraut, J., & Muschert, G.W. (2019). *Columbine, 20 Years Later and Beyond: Lessons from Tragedy* (p. 57). Santa Barbara, CA: Praeger.
17. (Scholdkraut & Muschert, 2019, p. 58)
18. Loreno, D., & Steer, J. (2018, March 1). Jackson Township student who shot self planned school shooting. *FOX 8 Cleveland.* Retrieved from https://fox8.com/2018/03/01/jackson-township-police-chief-to-hold-press-conference-regarding-last-weeks-middle-school-shooting/
19. Garrett, A. (2018, November 10). Man wounded in accidental shooting at UA dorm. *Akron Beacon Journal.* Retrieved from https://www.ohio.com/news/20181110/man-wounded-in-accidental-shooting-at-ua-dorm
20. L.A. middle school shooting suspect believed to be 12-year-old girl, police say. (2018, February 1). *Washington Times, The.* Retrieved from https://www.washingtontimes.com/news/2018/feb/1/salvador-b-castro-middle-school-shooting-suspect-1/
21. The latest: police say middle school shooting was accident. (2018, February 1). *Daily Herald.* Retrieved from https://www.dailyherald.com/article/20180201/news/302019886
22. Bode, N., Marzulli, J., & Williams, J. (2002, January 19). Cops grab suspect in school shootings. *Daily News (New York, New York)* (p. 4). Retrieved from https://www.newspapers.com/image/408356222/?terms=%22Vincent%2BRodriguez%22
23. (Bode, N., Marzulli, J., & Williams, 2002, p. 4)

24. Arrest in NYC school shooting. (2002, January 15). *CBS News*. Retrieved from https://www.cbsnews.com/news/arrest-in-nyc-school-shooting/
25. National Gang Center. (n.d.). *OJJDP comprehensive gang model*. Retrieved from https://www.nationalgangcenter.gov/comprehensive-gang-model
26. U.S. Department of Homeland Security. (2014, January). *Building communities of trust fact sheet* [PDF file]. Retrieved from https://www.dhs.gov/sites/default/files/publications/Building%20Communities%20of%20Trust.pdf
27. National Center for Healthy Safe Children. (2018). *Safe schools/healthy students*. Retrieved from https://healthysafechildren.org/grantee/safe-schools-healthy-students
28. E. Ky. man sentenced to 3 life terms in slayings. (2014, June 6). *WLKY Louisville*. Retrieved from https://www.wlky.com/article/e-ky-man-sentenced-to-3-life-terms-in-slayings/3750296
29. Estep, B., & Honeycutt Spears, V. (2013, January 16). 12-year-old girl becomes third to die from shooting at Hazard college. *Lexington Herald Leader*. Retrieved from https://www.kentucky.com/news/local/crime/article44397759.html
30. (Estep & Honeycutt Spears, 2013)
31. Frontline: the killer at Thurston High. (1998, May 20-21). *PBS*. Retrieved from https://www.pbs.org/wgbh/pages/frontline/shows/kinkel/kip/cron.html
32. (Frontline: the killer at Thurston High, 1998)
33. 8 years later: Thurston and Kinkel revisited. (2006, October 1). *Daily Emerald*. Retrieved from https://www.dailyemerald.com/archives/years-later-thurston-and-kinkel-revisited/article_d898f051-9e58-5621-9417-3d21f4ec946a.html
34. Everytown for Gun Safety Support Fund. (2016). *Analysis of school shootings* [PDF file] (p. 1). Retrieved from https://everytownresearch.org/documents/2015/04/analysis-of-school-shootings.pdf
35. Brantley, M. (2017, August 17). Judge opens dispositions of shooters in Westside case in 1998. *Arkansas Times*. Retrieved from https://www.arktimes.com/ArkansasBlog/archives/2017/08/15/judge-opens-depositions-of-shooters-in-westside-case-in-1998
36. Roberts, J. (2005, August 11). 'No Justice In This Whatsoever.' *CBS News*. Retrieved from https://www.cbsnews.com/news/no-justice-in-this-whatsoever/
37. Habersham, R. (2018, May 22). Child accidentally shot woman in school parking lot, authorities say. *Atlanta Journal-Constitution*. Retrieved from https://www.ajc.com/news/crime--law/child-accidentally-shot-woman-school-parking-lot-authorities-say/4Gyiorh3eTscRRCVpxERAO/
38. (Habersham, 2018)
39. Pugh, J. (2018, November 13). Suspects steal guns and ammunition from deputies patrol car. *WCBD – TV*. Retrieved from https://www.counton2.com/

news/local-news/suspects-steal-guns-and-ammunition-from-deputies-patrol-car/1594737367

40. Geranios, N. K. (2017, September 14). Victim told suspect in Washington school shooting: I knew you would 'shoot up the school.' *Chicago Tribune*. Retrieved from http://www.chicagotribune.com/news/nationworld/ct-washington-school-shooting-20170914-story.html

41. Blankstein, A., & Siemaszko, C. (2017, September 14). Washington school shooting suspect wanted to teach bullies a 'lesson.' *NBC News*. Retrieved from https://www.nbcnews.com/news/us-news/washington-school-shooting-suspect-wanted-teach-bullies-lesson-n801346

42. Geranios, N. K. (2017, September 14). Victim told suspect in Washington school shooting: I knew you would 'shoot up the school.' *Chicago Tribune*. Retrieved from http://www.chicagotribune.com/news/nationworld/ct-washington-school-shooting-20170914-story.html

43. (Geranios, 2017)

44. Trumka, R. (2024, February 22). Biometric gunsafes malfunction, allowing anyone to open; CPSC Widens Recall to 120,000 more safes sold by 4 manufacturers at Walmart, Amazon, and Bass Pro Shops; serious risk of death. *United States Consumer Product Safety Commission*. Retrieved from https://www.cpsc.gov/About-CPSC/Commissioner/Richard-Trumka/Statement/Biometric-Gunsafes-Malfunction-Allowing-Anyone-to-Open-CPSC-Widens-Recall-to-120000-More-Safes-Sold-by-4-Manufacturers-at-Walmart-Amazon-and-Bass-Pro-Shops-Serious-Risk-of-Death

45. Trumka, R. (2023, October 19). Malfunctioning gun safes sold by Cabela's, Bass Pro, and Lowe's allow anyone to open; one child dead. *United States Consumer Product Safety Commission*. Retrieved from https://www.cpsc.gov/About-CPSC/Commissioner/Richard-Trumka/Statement/Malfunctioning-Gun-Safes-Sold-by-Cabela%E2%80%99s-Bass-Pro-and-Lowe%E2%80%99s-Allow-Anyone-to-Open-One-Child-Dead

46. Gun used in Nevada teacher killing wasn't locked away: shooter's parents. (2013, November 7). *New York Daily News*. Retrieved from https://www.nydailynews.com/news/national/gun-nevada-teacher-shooting-wasn-locked-article-1.1509274

47. 12-year-old Nevada middle school shooter was bullied, left two suicide notes: police. (2014, March 14). *Daily News*. Retrieved from https://www.nydailynews.com/news/national/nevada-middle-school-shooter-left-2-suicide-notes-cops-article-1.1791820

48. Elam, S., Hanna, J., & Vercammen, P. (2013, October 25). 'Please don't shoot': Wounded survivor, 12, recalls Nevada school attack. *CNN*. Retrieved from https://www.cnn.com/2013/10/24/justice/nevada-school-shooting-survivor/

49. United States Secret Service & United States Department of Education. (2004, July). *The final report and findings of the safe school initiative: implications for the prevention of school attacks in the United States* [PDF file] (p. 27). Retrieved from https://www2.ed.gov/admins/lead/safety/preventingattacksreport.pdf
50. McCarthy/Santee, T. (2001, March 11). Warning: Andy Williams here. Unhappy kid. Tired of being picked on. *Time.* Retrieved from https://content.time.com/time/subscriber/article/0,33009,999474-1,00.html
51. Langman Ph.D., P. (2014). Charles Andrew Williams: sorting out the contradictions [PDF file]. *SchoolShooters.info* (p. 3). Retrieved from https://schoolshooters.info/sites/default/files/williams_contradictions_1.1.pdf
52. McCarthy/Santee, T. (2001, March 11). Warning: Andy Williams here. Unhappy kid. Tired of being picked on. *Time.* Retrieved from https://content.time.com/time/subscriber/article/0,33009,999474-1,00.html
53. (McCarthy/Santee, 2001)
54. School shooting sentencing. (2002, August 15). *CNN.* Retrieved from http://transcripts.cnn.com/TRANSCRIPTS/0208/15/se.08.html
55. Demer, L. (2017, February 18). Evan Ramsey's tattered life filled him with rage. Then he brought a shotgun to school. *Anchorage Daily News.* Retrieved from https://www.adn.com/alaska-news/2017/02/18/evan-ramseys-tattered-life-filled-him-with-rage-then-he-brought-a-shotgun-to-school/
56. Fainaru, S. (1998, October 19). A tragedy was preceded by many overlooked signals. *Boston Globe, The* (p. A10). Retrieved from https://www.newspapers.com/image/441992217/?terms=%2C%2Btragedy%2Bwas%2Bpreceded%2Bby%2Bmany%2Boverlooked%2Bsignals
57. Newman, K.S., Fox, C., Harding, D., Mehta, J., & Roth, W. (2004). *Rampage: the social roots of school shootings* (p. 155). New York, NY: Basic Books.
58. Fainaru, S. (1998, October 19). A tragedy was preceded by many overlooked signals. *Boston Globe, The* (p. A11). Retrieved from https://www.newspapers.com/image/441992217/?terms=%2C%2Btragedy%2Bwas%2Bpreceded%2Bby%2Bmany%2Boverlooked%2Bsignals
59. Shapiro, E. (2017, March 27). Maryland teen was plotting mass school shooting, police say. *ABC News.* Retrieved from https://abcnews.go.com/US/maryland-teen-plotting-mass-school-shooting-police/story?id=46404763
60. Maryland teen sentenced to 20 years in alleged school bomb plot. (2018, January 31). *Associated Press and NBC Washington.* Retrieved from https://www.nbcwashington.com/news/local/Teen-Sentenced-to-20-Years-in-Alleged-School-Attack-Plot-471906243.html
61. (Maryland teen sentenced, 2018)
62. Cops credit parents with thwarting school attack plot. (2017, March 27). *CBS News.* Retrieved from https://www.cbsnews.com/news/cops-credit-parents-with-thwarting-school-attack-plot/

63. Mom turns in son after finding school shooting plot in journal. (2019, October 7, 2019). *WFMY-TV*. Retrieved from https://www.wfmynews2.com/article/news/nation-world/mom-turns-in-son-for-school-shooting-plot-in-journal-columbine-anniversary/83-ed0a16a8-2299-4ba4-b960-44fcbdc38f92
64. Fortin, J., & Smith, M. (2018, March 3). Central Michigan University gunman was acting oddly before shooting, police say. *New York Times, The*. Retrieved from https://www.nytimes.com/2018/03/03/us/central-michigan-shooting.html
65. Sanchez, R., & Watts, A. (2018, March 3). Son arrested in shooting deaths of parents at Central Michigan University. *CNN*. Retrieved from https://www.cnn.com/2018/03/02/us/central-michigan-university-shots-fired/index.html
66. Rubin, J. (2012, April 3). 7 shot dead in Oakland campus rampage. *Los Angeles Times*. Retrieved from https://www.latimes.com/archives/la-xpm-2012-apr-03-la-me-oakland-college-shooting-20120403-story.html
67. Gwynne, K. (2014, July 14). School shootings: widely reported tragedies since 2000. *Rolling Stone*. Retrieved from https://www.rollingstone.com/culture/culture-lists/school-shootings-widely-reported-tragedies-since-2000-19794/march-21st-2005-red-lake-high-school-64556/
68. Allen, N. (2012, April 4). US college killer lined up his victims and then shot them at point blank range. *Irish Independent*. Retrieved from https://www.independent.ie/news/us-college-killer-lined-up-his-victims-and-then-shot-them-at-point-blank-range/26839415.html
69. Johnson, S. (2016, July 20). Anniversary of Oikos shooting massacre in Oakland evokes painful memories. *Eastbay Times*. Retrieved from https://www.eastbaytimes.com/2013/03/30/anniversary-of-oikos-shooting-massacre-in-oakland-evokes-painful-memories/
70. (Johnson, 2016)
71. Three teens injured in Champaign shooting released from hospital. (2017, December 10). *Herald & Review*. Retrieved from https://herald-review.com/news/state-and-regional/three-teens-injured-in-champaign-shooting-released-from-hospital/article_b3c5d86a-5aa2-575e-b672-79654213fba4.html
72. Schenk, M. (2020, January 9). Two years on, no answers about shooting at Central after basketball game. *News-Gazette, The*. Retrieved from https://www.news-gazette.com/sports/prep-sports/boys-basketball/two-years-on-no-answers-about-shooting-at-central-after-basketball-game/article_83ca30b3-4771-5d97-86bc-1c4759de7977.html
73. Moore, M. H., Petrie, C. V., Braga, A. A., & McLaughlin, B. L. (2003). *Deadly lessons: understanding lethal school violence* (p. 186). Washington, D.C.: The National Academy Press.
74. (Moore et al.,2003, p. 186)

75. (Moore et al., 2003, p. 187)
76. Wilson, T. (1994, January 22). Teen guilty of slaying in Tilden High hallway. *Chicago Tribune*. Retrieved from https://www.chicagotribune.com/news/ct-xpm-1994-01-22-9401220160-story.html
77. Moore, M. H., Petrie, C. V., Braga, A. A., & McLaughlin, B. L. (2003). *Deadly lessons: understanding lethal school violence* (p. 188). Washington, D.C.: The National Academy Press.
78. Christoff, C. (1998, February 27). Suicide at school shocks small town. *Detroit Free Press* (p. 1B). Retrieved from https://www.newspapers.com/image/100151213
79. Eighth-grader kills himself in Osceola County middle school. (1998, February 27). *Central Michigan Life* [PDF file] (p. 2). Retrieved from https://cmuhistory.cmich.edu/?a=d&d=IsabellaCML19980227&e=-------en-10--1--txt-txIN--------
80. (Eighth-grader kills himself, 1998, p. 6B)
81. Redden, J. (2014, December 24). Police: Recovered gun used in shooting near school. *Portland Tribune*. Retrieved from https://pamplinmedia.com/pt/9-news/244918-112711-police-recovered-gun-used-in-shooting-near-school
82. Green, A. (2019, January 9). Teen who shot four at Rosemary Anderson High gets 10 years; co-defendants get 7 and 8 years. *Oregonian, The*. Retrieved from https://www.oregonlive.com/portland/2015/05/teen_who_shot_four_outside_ros.html
83. Three sentenced in Rosemary Anderson HS shooting. (2015, May 13). *KGW8*. Retrieved from https://www.kgw.com/article/news/crime/three-sentenced-in-rosemary-anderson-hs-shooting/67280521
84. Bernstein, M. (2015, January 19). Killingsworth shooting: Fourth man accused of hindering prosecution. *Oregonian, The*. Retrieved from https://www.oregonlive.com/portland/2015/01/killingsworth_shooting_fourth.html
85. Three sentenced in Rosemary Anderson HS shooting. (2015, May 13). *KGW8*. Retrieved from https://www.kgw.com/article/news/crime/three-sentenced-in-rosemary-anderson-hs-shooting/67280521
86. Kelley, B. (2008, March 28). Savannah State University adds more security on campus. *WTOC11*. Retrieved from https://www.wtoc.com/story/8085345/savannah-state-university-adds-more-security-on-campus/
87. James, A. (2015, August 28). SSU security heightened at gates throughout weekend. *WSAV*. Retrieved from https://www.wsav.com/news/ssu-security-heightened-at-gates-throughout-weekend/
88. LaBrot, A. (2018, February 27). Savannah State University officials speak publicly; students want more. *WTOC11*. Retrieved from https://www.wtoc.com/story/37606097/savannah-state-president-discusses-campus-safety-measures-after-fatal-shooting-this-past-weekend/

89. Gilbert, A. (2019, September 16). SSU implements new Visitor Center, security measures. *Savannah Morning News*. Retrieved from https://www.savannahnow.com/story/news/2019/09/17/savannah-state-implements-new-visitor-center-security-measures/2752680007/

90. Moorman, B. (2022, April 23). Police: two injured in Friday night shooting on Savannah State campus; GBI investigating. *Savannah Morning News*. Retrieved from https://www.savannahnow.com/story/news/crime/2022/04/23/shooting-savannah-state-university-police-two-injured-friday-night/7422570001/

91. Hamilton, E. (2022, April 24). 2 shot at Savannah State University, GBI called in to investigate. *WJCL Savannah*. Retrieved from https://www.wjcl.com/article/shot-savannah-state-university-gbi-police-investigating/39802660

92. Ford, B. (2009, May 22). Harlem man arrested in murder at Harvard is son of retired NYPD cop. *Daily News*. Retrieved from https://www.nydailynews.com/news/crime/harlem-man-arrested-murder-harvard-son-retired-nypd-article-1.410465

93. Newcomer, E. P., & Srivatsa, N. N. (2010, September 22). Suicide Note Found Online. *The Harvard Crimson*. Retrieved from https://www.thecrimson.com/article/2010/9/22/heisman-harvard-mother-death/

94. 18-year-old charged in Dunbar High shootings. (2009, January 16). *NBC Chicago*. Retrieved from https://www.nbcchicago.com/local/18-year-old-charged-in-dunbar-high-shootings/1854988/

95. People v. Dukes, 2015 Ill. App. 130881 (Ill. App. Ct. 2015). Retrieved from https://casetext.com/case/people-v-dukes-124

96. $2 million bail in shooting. (2021, August 22). *Chicago Tribune*. Retrieved from https://www.chicagotribune.com/2009/01/17/2-million-bail-in-shooting-2/

97. People v. Dukes, 2015 Ill. App. 130881 (Ill. App. Ct. 2015). Retrieved from https://casetext.com/case/people-v-dukes-124

98. Wilson, N., Holliman, A. R., & Hall, C. (2024, June 25). What are community violence intervention programs? *Center for American Progress*. Retrieved from https://www.americanprogress.org/article/what-are-community-violence-intervention-programs/?utm_source=chatgpt.com

99. (Wilson et al., 2024)

100. Cure Violence Global. (2022, August). *The evidence of effectiveness* [PDF file] (pp. 6-7). Retrieved from https://cvg.org/wp-content/uploads/2022/09/Cure-Violence-Evidence-Summary.pdf

101. Everytown for Gun Safety Support Fund. (2022, December 9). *Community-led public safety strategies*. Retrieved from https://everytownresearch.org/report/community-led-public-safety-strategies/

102. U.S. Department of Justice. (2024, June 25). *Fact sheet: two years of the Bipartisan Safer Communities Act*. Retrieved from https://www.justice.gov/opa/pr/fact-sheet-two-years-bipartisan-safer-communities-act

103. U.S. Department of Justice Office of Justice Programs. (2024, March 22). *Community violence intervention: a collaborative approach to addressing community violence.* Retrieved from https://www.ojp.gov/archive/topics/community-violence-intervention
104. Bureau of Justice Assistance. (2022, April). *Community based violence intervention and prevention initiative implementation checklist* [PDF file]. Retrieved from https://www.ojp.gov/sites/g/files/xyckuh241/files/media/document/cvi-implementation-checklist_0.pdf

Chapter 13: To Ban or Not to Ban AR-15s

1. Epstein, K. (2023, June 28). Scot Peterson did not confront the Parkland school shooting. Should he be jailed? *BBC*. Retrieved from https://www.bbc.com/news/world-us-canada-65994768
2. Méndez, M. (2023, May 24). Uvalde school shooting: What we know one year later. *The Texas Tribune*. Retrieved from https://www.texastribune.org/2023/05/24/uvalde-school-shooting-what-to-know/

Chapter 14: Alyssa's Law

1. What is Alyssa's Law? (2024). *Make Our Schools Safe*. Retrieved from https://makeourschoolssafe.org/alyssas-law/
2. King, B. (2024, February 2024). Mom 'never giving up' after Virginia lawmakers vote to table Alyssa's law. *WTVR CBS 6 Richmond*. Retrieved from https://www.wtvr.com/news/local-news/alyssas-law-february-8-2024

Chapter 16: Apps That Can Help Save Children's Lives

1. Wyllie, D. (2021, August 3). New app cuts response time to active shooter attacks. *Police Magazine*. Retrieved from https://www.policemag.com/technology/article/15310096/new-app-cuts-response-time-to-active-shooter-attacks
2. Mascarenhas, L. (2024, April 20). Experts say panic buttons can enhance school safety, but only 6 states require them. *CNN*. Retrieved from https://www.cnn.com/2024/04/20/us/panic-buttons-schools-us-states/index.html
3. Guard911 Comparison. (2025). *Guard911*. Retrieved from https://guard911.com/features/
4. Alyssa's Law & Security Compliance. (2025). *SaferWatch*. Retrieved from https://www.saferwatchapp.com/products/mobile-panic-alert-system/

Chapter Sample of Author's Next Book

This chapter sample is from *The Ultimate U.S. School Shooting Reference Guide, Volume 1: 1990-1999*. This book meticulously documents every known school shooting in the United States during the 1990s, offering detailed accounts of hundreds of incidents. Authored by Luis D. Aponte, a librarian and U.S. Air Force veteran, the guide identifies patterns and causes behind these tragedies, aiming to foster understanding and inspire solutions to prevent future violence. With comprehensive data and insights, it serves as a vital resource for researchers, parents, community members, educators, and policymakers dedicated to creating safer schools.

962
Location of shooting: Columbine High School
Date: 4/20/1999
City, State: Littleton, CO
Name of victim(s) killed: Cassie Bernall, Steven Curnow, Corey DePooter, Kelly Fleming, Matthew Kechter, Daniel Mauser, Daniel Rohrbough, William "Dave" Sanders, Rachel Scott, Isaiah Shoels, John Tomlin, Lauren Townsend, Kyle Velasquez, Eric Harris (shooter), and Dylan Klebold (shooter).

Age of victim(s) killed: 17, 14, 17, 16, 16, 15, 15, 47, 17, 18, 16, 18, 16, 18, & 17

Name of victim(s) injured: Evan Todd, Sean Graves, Mark Taylor, Michael (Mike) Johnson, Makai Hall, Lance Kirklin, Nicole Nowlen, Adam Kyler, Richard Castaldo, Mark Kintgen, Patrick Ireland, Kasey Ruegsegger, Jennifer Doyle, Stephanie Munson, Danny (Dan) Steepleton, Brian Anderson, Valeen Schnurr, Lisa Kreutz, Jeanna Park, Nicholas (Nick) Foss, Joyce Jankowski, Patricia (Pat) Nielson, Stephen Austin Eubanks, unreported, unreported, unreported, and unreported.

Age of victim(s) injured: 15, 15, 15, 15, 16, 16, 16, 16, 17, 17, 17, 17, 17, 17, 17, 18, 18, 18, 18, 45, 45, unreported, unreported, unreported, unreported, & unreported.

Name of suspect(s)/shooter(s): Eric Harris and Dylan Klebold.

Age of suspect(s)/shooter(s): 18 & 17

Weapon(s): Intratec TEC-DC9 semi-automatic pistol, Hi-Point 995 Carbine pistol, Savage 67H pump-action shotgun, Stevens 311D double barreled sawed-off shotgun, 100 rounds of ammunition, 99 explosives, and 4 knives.

High capacity magazine(s)?: Yes. No details mentioned.

Weapon(s) legally acquired by suspect(s)/shooter(s)?: No. Illegally purchased by shooters from Mark Manes, who was sentenced to six years in prison.

# of people killed: 16

# of people injured: 27

Total # of victims: 43

Time suspect(s)/shooter(s) were apprehended or killed?: Suicide. Shooters committed suicide approximately 49 minutes after shooting began.

Suspect(s)' mental illness: Eric Haris complained of depression, anger, and suicidal thoughts to psychiatrist.

Suspect(s)' medication or drug use: Eric Harris had been taking Luvox for a year and a half, prior to school attack.

Suspect(s)' criminal history: Both suspects were arrested in January 1998 for theft. Pled guilty and sent to a juvenile diversion program.

Warning signs: Shooter's sister claimed he "joked around in class about shooting people. He acted like he had a gun, but no one took him seriously." Eric Harris' journal entries express his admiration for Nazis and swastikas, his admission of being a racist, his hatred of his own appearance, his lack of self-esteem, and his desire to kill and instill fear in others.

Suspect(s)' country of citizenship: U.S.A.

Suspect(s)' religious affiliation: Unreported.

Alleged reason for shooting: Bullying. Physical and verbal. Psychopathic behavior.

Metal detectors present?: Unreported.

Location & time of shooting: The suspects placed a 20-pound propane bomb in the cafeteria at 11:10 a.m., then began shooting students in the library and hallways around 11:19 a.m. before killing themselves in the school's library at approximately 12:08 p.m.

For more information, contact: Judge Robert Blackburn, Colorado Attorney General Ken Salazar, Psychiatrist Dr. Frank Ochberg, and FBI Supervisory Special Agent Dwayne Fuselier.

Citations/sources: (Columbine Shooting, 2018) (Landman, 2013, p. 5) (National School Safety Center, 2010, p. 22 & 23) (Crews, 2016, p. 6) (Lebrun, 2009, p. 175) (Newman, Fox, Harding, Mehta, & Roth, 2004, p. 139, 238, & 247) (Fleshler, Chokey, Huriash & Trischitta, 2018, p. 1A & 9A) (Columbine High School, 2019) (Cullen, 2004) (Cabell: Columbine killers, 2003) (Levenson, 2025) (Conditions of school shooting victims, 1999) (Conditions of the wounded, 1999) (Obmascik, 2019) (Ontiveroz, 2019)

#961

Location of shooting: Martin Luther King Jr. Middle School

Date: 4/22/1999

City, State: Atlanta, GA

Name of victim(s) killed: Geno Vaelette Jerome Thomas.

Age of victim(s) killed: 13

Name of victim(s) injured: N/A.

Age of victim(s) injured: N/A.

Name of suspect(s)/shooter(s): Horace "Bubba" Holt Jr.

Age of suspect(s)/shooter(s): 17

Weapon(s): Revolver.

High capacity magazine(s)?: Unreported.

Weapon(s) legally acquired by suspect(s)/shooter(s)?: No.

# of people killed: 1

# of people injured: 0

Total # of victims: 1

Time suspect(s)/shooter(s) were apprehended or killed?: Suspect turned himself in two days after the shooting.

Suspect(s)' mental illness: Unreported.

Suspect(s)' medication or drug use: Unreported.

Suspect(s)' criminal history: Suspect was previously arrested for fighting, but was given a copy of the charges instead of being booked into jail.

Warning signs: Unreported.

Suspect(s)' country of citizenship: Unreported.

Suspect(s)' religious affiliation: Unreported.

Alleged reason for shooting: Unreported.

Metal detectors present?: N/A.

Location & time of shooting: Victim was shot in a parking lot next to the school at 9:45 p.m., after a school jazz and dance recital.

For more information, contact: Homicide Squad Supervisor Sgt. Cecil Mann, Maj. Mickey Lloyd, Mayor Bill Campbell, Atlanta Homicide Sgt. Scott Bennett, Detectives Bret Zimbrick, Dale Kelly, and A.B. Calhoun.

Citations/sources: (Carter, 2000) (National School Safety Center, 2010, p. 23) (Carter & Ffrench-Parker, 1999, p. G1 & G6) (Warner, 1999, p. F1)

Location of shooting: Scotlandville Middle School

Date: 4/22/1999

City, State: Scotlandville, LA

Name of victim(s) killed: N/A.

Age of victim(s) killed: N/A.

Name of victim(s) injured: Unnamed girl due to age.

Age of victim(s) injured: 14

Name of suspect(s)/shooter(s): Murphy Young (shooter) and Jonathan Wells (accomplice).

Age of suspect(s)/shooter(s): 14 & 14

Weapon(s): .22-caliber pistol.

High capacity magazine(s)?: Unreported.

Weapon(s) legally acquired by suspect(s)/shooter(s)?: No.

# of people killed: 0

# of people injured: 1

Total # of victims: 1

Time suspect(s)/shooter(s) were apprehended or killed?: Suspect was arrested within hours of the shooting.

Suspect(s)' mental illness: Unreported.

Suspect(s)' medication or drug use: Unreported.

Suspect(s)' criminal history: Young had previously been arrested for having a gun near a school campus.

Warning signs: Unreported.

Suspect(s)' country of citizenship: Unreported.

Suspect(s)' religious affiliation: Unreported.

Alleged reason for shooting: Argument.

Metal detectors present?: N/A.

Location & time of shooting: Victim was shot outside, between two school buildings at about 12:30 p.m. Suspect shot the wrong student from 100 yards away.

For more information, contact: East Baton Rouge Parish Sheriff's Office Lt. Darrell Oneal and Baton Rouge General Medical Center Spokeswoman Jace Dobrowolski.

Citations/sources: (Teen-age girl is wounded, 1999, p. 17A) (School incidents probed, 1999, p. 2)

#959
Location of shooting: Heritage High School
Date: 5/20/1999
City, State: Conyers, GA
Name of victim(s) killed: N/A.
Age of victim(s) killed: N/A.
Name of victim(s) injured: Drake Hoy, Ryan Rosa, Jason Cheek, Brian Barnhardt, Cania Collins, and Stephanie Laster.
Age of victim(s) injured: 18, 18, 17, 16, 15, & 15
Name of suspect(s)/shooter(s): Anthony B. "T.J." Solomon, Jr.
Age of suspect(s)/shooter(s): 15
Weapon(s): .22-caliber rifle and .357 magnum revolver.
High capacity magazine(s)?: No. Standard 12-round rifle.
Weapon(s) legally acquired by suspect(s)/shooter(s)?: No. Stolen from his step-father's locked gun cabinet.
# of people killed: 0
# of people injured: 6
Total # of victims: 6
Time suspect(s)/shooter(s) were apprehended or killed?: Shooter surrendered firearm to principal within 12 minutes of shooting.
Suspect(s)' mental illness: Yes. Attention deficit disorder. Diagnosed with clinical depression -- possibly dysthymic disorder.
Suspect(s)' medication or drug use: Ritalin.
Suspect(s)' criminal history: None.
Warning signs: Shooter brought a gun to school a month before the shooting and showed it to a friend who then reported him to the school office. Told friends he was going to shoot his classmates. Threatened to blow up his classroom. Suicidal threats.
Suspect(s)' country of citizenship: U.S.A.
Suspect(s)' religious affiliation: Christian

<u>Alleged reason for shooting</u>: Mental illness, rejection and influence from Columbine shooting. Distraught over a breakup with his girlfriend.

<u>Metal detectors present?</u>: Unreported.

<u>Location & time of shooting</u>: Shooting occurred in one of the common areas of the school approximately 7:30 a.m.

<u>For more information, contact</u>: Former Assistant Principal Cecil Brinkley, Rockdale County District Attorney Richard Read, Forensic Psychologist James Edwards, and Juvenile Judge Court Judge William Schneider.

<u>Citations/sources</u>: (Moore, Petrie, Braga, & McLaughlin, 2003, p.25, 38-40, 52, 54, 266-283) (Queen, 2016) (Cloud, 1999) (Lebrun, 2009, p. 175) (Newman, Fox, Harding, Mehta, & Roth, 2004, p. 238) (Stafford, 2000, p. JR5) (Stafford, 1999, p. C1 & C6) (Jones, 1999, p. 1A & 2A) (Quinn, 2015)

#958

<u>Location of shooting</u>: Jasper County Comprehensive High School
<u>Date</u>: 8/25/1999
<u>City, State</u>: Monticello, GA
<u>Name of victim(s) killed</u>: Amanda Gaylynne Tanquary (shooter).
<u>Age of victim(s) killed</u>: 16
<u>Name of victim(s) injured</u>: N/A.
<u>Age of victim(s) injured</u>: N/A.
<u>Name of suspect(s)/shooter(s)</u>: Amanda Gaylynne Tanquary.
<u>Age of suspect(s)/shooter(s)</u>: 16
<u>Weapon(s)</u>: Unreported.
<u>High capacity magazine(s)?</u>: Unreported.
<u>Weapon(s) legally acquired by suspect(s)/shooter(s)?</u>: No.
<u># of people killed</u>: 1
<u># of people injured</u>: 0
<u>Total # of victims</u>: 1
<u>Time suspect(s)/shooter(s) were apprehended or killed?</u>: Suicide.
<u>Suspect(s)' mental illness</u>: Unreported.

<u>Suspect(s)' medication or drug use</u>: Unreported.
<u>Suspect(s)' criminal history</u>: Unreported.
<u>Warning signs</u>: Unreported.
<u>Suspect(s)' country of citizenship</u>: Unreported.
<u>Suspect(s)' religious affiliation</u>: Unreported.
<u>Alleged reason for shooting</u>: Unreported.
<u>Metal detectors present?</u>: N/A.
<u>Location & time of shooting</u>: Student shot herself in a pickup truck parked in the school parking lot. Her body was discovered shortly after 9:00 a.m.
<u>For more information, contact</u>: Jasper County Superintendent Julian Cope, Student Services Director Mike Newton, and Jasper County Emergency Management Director Ed Westbrook.
<u>Citations/sources</u>: (National School Safety Center, 2010, p. 23) (Williams, 1999a, p. A-8)

#957
Location of shooting: Vines High School
<u>Date</u>: 9/7/1999
<u>City, State</u>: Plano, TX
<u>Name of victim(s) killed</u>: Brent Austin (shooter)
<u>Age of victim(s) killed</u>: 16
<u>Name of victim(s) injured</u>: N/A.
<u>Age of victim(s) injured</u>: N/A.
<u>Name of suspect(s)/shooter(s)</u>: Brent Austin
<u>Age of suspect(s)/shooter(s)</u>: 16
<u>Weapon(s)</u>: Small caliber handgun.
<u>High capacity magazine(s)?</u>: Unreported.
<u>Weapon(s) legally acquired by suspect(s)/shooter(s)?</u>: No. Gun stolen from parents.
<u># of people killed</u>: 1
<u># of people injured</u>: 0
<u>Total # of victims</u>: 1
<u>Time suspect(s)/shooter(s) were apprehended or killed?</u>: Suicide.

Suspect(s)' mental illness: Unreported.
Suspect(s)' medication or drug use: Unreported.
Suspect(s)' criminal history: Unreported.
Warning signs: Unreported.
Suspect(s)' country of citizenship: Unreported.
Suspect(s)' religious affiliation: Unreported.
Alleged reason for shooting: Unreported.
Metal detectors present?: Unreported.
Location & time of shooting: Student shot himself in school boy's bathroom stall about 12:30 p.m.
For more information, contact: Plano Police Spokesman Carl Duke.
Citations/sources: (National School Safety Center, 2010, p. 23) (Muscanere, 1999a, p. 1A) (Muscanere, 1999b, p. 1A)

#956
Location of shooting: Santa Teresa High School
Date: 9/9/1999
City, State: San Jose, CA
Name of victim(s) killed: Marcos Sarabia (shooter).
Age of victim(s) killed: 16
Name of victim(s) injured: N/A.
Age of victim(s) injured: N/A.
Name of suspect(s)/shooter(s): Marcos Sarabia
Age of suspect(s)/shooter(s): 16
Weapon(s): Handgun.
High capacity magazine(s)?: Unreported.
Weapon(s) legally acquired by suspect(s)/shooter(s)?: No.
# of people killed: 1
# of people injured: 0
Total # of victims: 1
Time suspect(s)/shooter(s) were apprehended or killed?: Suicide.
Suspect(s)' mental illness: Unreported.
Suspect(s)' medication or drug use: Unreported.

<u>Suspect(s)' criminal history</u>: None.
<u>Warning signs</u>: No.
<u>Suspect(s)' country of citizenship</u>: Unreported.
<u>Suspect(s)' religious affiliation</u>: Unreported.
<u>Alleged reason for shooting</u>: Unreported.
<u>Metal detectors present?</u>: No.
<u>Location & time of shooting</u>: Student shot himself in school bathroom at approximately 8:20 a.m.

<u>For more information, contact</u>: San Jose Acting Deputy Chief Donald Anders, Superintendent Joe Coto, and Deputy District Superintendent Bill Kugler.

<u>Citations/sources</u>: (National School Safety Center, 2010, p. 24) (Teen kills self in San Jose, 1999, p. A-5) (Squatriglia, Lynem, & Gaura, 1999)

www.ingramcontent.com/pod-product-compliance
Lightning Source LLC
Chambersburg PA
CBHW041039050426

42337CB00059B/5075